W9-DDC-110

THE LIBRARY
COLBY JUNIOR COLLEGE

IN MEMORY OF
Edith Long

GRÜNEWALD

GRÜNEWALD

NIKOLAUS PEVSNER

MICHAEL MEIER

---

117 PHOTOGRAVURE PLATES

26 COLOUR PLATES

HARRY N. ABRAMS INC · NEW YORK

ND
588
G7
P4

#F 12.31 Eastern 3/18/64

LIBRARY OF CONGRESS CATALOG CARD NUMBER: 58–9033

ALL RIGHTS RESERVED
PUBLISHED IN THE UNITED STATES OF AMERICA IN 1958 BY
HARRY N. ABRAMS INC. NEW YORK
PRODUCED BY THAMES AND HUDSON LONDON AND ATLANTIS VERLAG ZÜRICH
TEXT PRINTED IN GREAT BRITAIN BY JARROLD AND SONS LTD NORWICH
COLOUR PLATES PRINTED BY BUCHDRUCKEREI BERICHTHAUS ZÜRICH
GRAVURE PLATES PRINTED BY GEBRÜDER FRETZ AG ZÜRICH

47399

CONTENTS

LIST OF PLATES

The numbers of the Colour Plates are given in italic

AN INTRODUCTION TO GRÜNEWALD'S ART

by Nikolaus Pevsner

I

The purpose of this book is to introduce the English-speaking public to one of the greatest masters of European painting, to the greatest painter Germany has produced, and one whose fame, in spite of that, goes back even in Germany no more than fifty years and whose real name has been known to us for no more than twenty. The name under which he appears in this book was not his, was in fact invented more than a century after his death, and yet will remain his—one more ambiguity in an ambiguous work, a work for ever attracting, for ever repelling.

There are few places in which Grünewald's painting can be seen, and there is only one where the full impact of his genius can be experienced. If no visit can be paid to the museum at Colmar, a journey through the plates in this book, both those in black-and-white and in colour, will do much. But Grünewald is an artist who cannot be fully understood except against his setting, his epoch, the artists in emu-lation of, and competition with, whom he worked; and Germany on the eve of the Reformation is, alas, as little known to Anglo-Saxons as Grünewald. Not even Dürer, who dominates this period in art as magisterially as Goethe dominated his in thought, can be taken for granted, in spite of paintings in two public galleries and engravings and woodcuts in many. And as for German sculpture, supreme among contemporary sculpture of all countries of the North, only the most modest experience of it can be presumed. So of all these things something will have to be related in these introductory pages. Then, when this has been done, they must also try to paraphrase Grünewald's art; for his art, haunting as it is, is a difficult art, difficult to take in visually and difficult to follow in its meanings.

II

Art on the eve of the Reformation—the term would mean little as applied to England, it means much as applied to Germany. In England, what could one think of? The sculptural decoration of Henry VII's Chapel at Westminster Abbey, the stained glass of King's College Chapel in Cambridge, the chancel-screen of York Minster, the painted screens of Norfolk churches—nothing that is of a Europeanly outstanding quality, and certainly nothing that would point specifically to the Reformation. In Germany all this is different; sculpture, painting and engraving all reached a superb climax in the years between 1480 and 1530, and all expressed the mood of the Reformation, of Humanism on the one side, of the spiritual revolution on the other. But who has ever heard of them in England, of the majesty and energy of Pacher's altarpiece at St Wolfgang, the fabulous jaggedness of Bernt Notke's dragon effort-lessly slain by St George, the almost painful intensity of the apostles in Veit Stoss's Cracow Altarpiece, all of about 1480; then of the Gothic classicity of Kraft, and the Italian classicity of the Vischers, and finally of the frenzy of Hans Leinberger and the maniac intricacy of the Breisach Altarpiece of the 1520's? Yet in this sculpture lie the sources of the angularity and the exquisite sparingness of Schongauer, Europe's greatest engraver of the last decades of the fifteenth century; in this sculpture also, at least partially, lie the sources of Dürer, who received his first training from a gold-smith (who happened to be his father), and of Grünewald too.

The quality of German woodcarving at the time of Grünewald is of the highest in Europe, higher than that of the Netherlands and far more exciting if not necessarily higher than that of the best French sculpture in stone. England has nothing to offer anywhere to compare with the *Dangolsheim Virgin* in the museum in Berlin or the choir-stalls of Ulm. Up to the time when they were carved—that is, up to about 1480 —German painting could hardly compete with German sculpture or indeed with the painting in other countries. There is no Eyck, no Campin, no Roger van der Weyden, no Hugo van der Goes, no Memling among German painters (as there is emphatically not among the painters of England). There is no Fouquet, no Master of the Roman du Cœur d'Amour épris, no Rohan-Master in German painting either. Konrad Witz, who came from Swabia and lived in Switzerland, that is, on the Burgundian border, is the only painter of considerable calibre. The rest are provin-cial, however much of interest and enjoyment the specialist's loving attention may discover. Dürer's master Wolgemut in Nuremberg certainly was provincial. Schongauer, the engraver, again working on the Burgundian border, was not; but when in 1491 Dürer, as a journeyman twenty years old, travelled to Colmar to meet him and no doubt to work under him, he had just died. Schongauer was primarily an engraver, not a painter. Of Wolgemut's large workshop the most memorable products are books with woodcuts. Dürer in 1492 settled for a while in Basle and worked as an illustrator there. The Germans were more attracted to woodcutting and engraving, arts of the line, than to painting, the art of colour.

In 1495 Dürer visited Venice. But the impact of the journey was less that of the fluid, rich and subtle painting of Giovanni Bellini than that of the country and the people he met on the journey. He draws the clothes worn by Venetian women and places them side by side with the fashions of Nuremberg, he draws the plan of a

Venetian house, and he paints a series of miraculously free water-colours of the scenery of the Tirol and the Brenner Pass. They are (after one solitary sketch of 1473 by Leonardo da Vinci) the earliest examples of the art of landscape in Europe—landscape not as individual motifs added to form the background to a figure piece, but landscape as a rendering of a totality. Here, in these private travel records, Dürer shows for the first time that he was capable of achievements in tone and colour as well as in line. However, his major task after his return was entirely un-Italian again—very large and monumental woodcuts, notably those for the *Apocalypse*. Their grandeur is indisputable, but it is the grandeur of the Gothic North, not of Italy. The convulsed passion of the years of Luther's youth pulses in them.

Dürer's greatness is the range of his art. In the two or three years between 1502 and 1504 he drew the amazingly accurate likeness of a hare, blades of grass in a field, an iris, but also the shocking head of a martyred Christ dying; he engraved the nudes of *Adam and Eve*, placed and measured according to Italian canons of posture and proportion, he engraved the scene of the *Nativity*, where the affectionate intricacy of mood matches the mastery in the exact rendering of materials, and he painted the large piece of the *Adoration of the Magi* in which the warm, strong, rich colours are as powerful as the contours. This range of Dürer's is unparalleled, even among the contemporary artists of the High Renaissance in Italy, and unparalleled amongst artists—once again except for Leonardo da Vinci—is Dürer's curiosity and the range of his intellectual pursuits. He published a book on perspective, a book on proportions, and one on the art of fortification, and he took a strong line in the religious struggles of his time.

Luther had joined the Austin Friars in 1505 and was ordained in 1507. He saw papal Rome in 1510 and, after his return home, the evils of letters of indulgence sold and bought. So in 1517 he made known his ninety-five theses against letters of indulgence; 1520 is the year of Luther's greatest writings, the writings which established a reformed Christian faith. In December he burnt publicly the papal bull against his teaching. In 1521 he disputed before the Emperor Charles V and, on his way back, was kidnapped by the elector of Saxony, and hidden to protect him from arrest. It was then that he translated the Bible. From 1522 he lived at Wittenberg, preaching and conducting the growing Reformation.

Dürer went to the Netherlands in 1520 to have his Imperial pension renewed by Charles V. While there the rumour reached him that Luther had been arrested, and his diary, which luckily survives, suddenly changes from notes on work sold, on curiosities seen and bought, and on visits paid and received, to several pages of prayer and admonition, of appeal to Erasmus, and denunciation of the pope: "Oh ye Christians, pray ye to God for help; for His judgment is near and His justice shall be revealed. Then we shall see the innocent bleed, whose blood has been shed by the pope, the priests and the monks and those whom they have judged and damned. Apocalypse. They are the slain, lying below the altar of God, and crying for revenge, whereon the voice of God answers: Await the full number of those that were slain innocently, then I shall judge." That was in 1521. In the same year the Anabaptists began to stir. Hans Denck, passionate enthusiast more then revolutionary, was expelled in 1525 from Nuremberg. In that year the Peasants' War broke out, a revolt half social and half religious. Luther, by then the accepted leader of reformed Christianity, preached violently against both. Dürer in 1526 painted his *Four Apostles* and presented them to the City Council of Nuremberg. They are an epitome of the German Renaissance—German as well as Renaissance: German in their exceeding intensity, Renaissance in their calm composition and monumental scale. Dürer provided them with long inscriptions warning "all secular rulers in these dangerous times to be watchful lest they mistake human thought for the word of God". Two years later on April 6, 1528, Dürer died, aged fifty-seven.

III

In August of the same year Grünewald died, probably about sixty-six or sixty-seven years old. He can never have been as famous as Dürer, or else his real name could not have been lost sight of so completely. The improbable story and all that is known of his life are related in the later pages of this book.

For an understanding of his art two facts from his life must here be emphasized. That he was a hydraulic engineer as well as a painter; that is, as competent a technician as Dürer (and Michelangelo, let alone Leonardo). And that he was, again like Dürer, a follower of Luther. He was dismissed from service under the elector of Mainz in 1526 and had among his belongings Lutheran tracts. But when he painted the Isenheim Altarpiece he cannot have been a Lutheran yet; for the altar was completed in 1515 or 1516, before Luther published his ninety-five theses in distant Wittenberg.

The artistic situation in those years, about 1512–16, was like this. Dürer had revisited Venice in 1505–6 or –7. This time Bellini's colour and open technique had meant all to him, and during and immediately after his stay he painted pictures more sensuous than any others of his (for instance, the portrait at Hampton Court). But once again the immediate impact wore off, and though his compositions for the rest of his life are grander and easier than they had been before, he remained primarily a master of the line, of drawing, woodcutting, engraving and etching. But Hans Burckmayr of Augsburg must also have gone to Venice during the same years as Dürer, and, the Augsburg of the Fugger being more internationally minded than Nuremberg, took more kindly to the pleasures of the Renaissance. Augsburg is the city where Holbein was born and educated. He lived at Basle before he went to England, and clearly knew Milan and Lombardy if not Venice.

For Grünewald no Italian journey is known, nor is one likely. But he knew Dürer, though he met him personally only in 1520, on October 23, at Aachen, when Dürer presented him with two florins-worth of his *Kunst*, which means of his engravings and woodcuts. Two florins-worth was much; for the whole *Engraved Passion* sold for ½ fl. and the whole big *Woodcut Passion* or the whole *Life of the Virgin* for ¼ fl. This shows much appreciation on Dürer's part. That Grünewald appreciated Dürer as well, we cannot prove by documents, though we can safely assume it. Dürer's prints were widely known; they travelled far—to Italy as well as to the Netherlands and England. Grünewald must have known Dürer as a painter too; for he was commissioned by Jacob Heller of Frankfurt to paint the wings of an altarpiece, the centre of which Dürer had delivered in 1509. The centre, one of Dürer's major works, was burnt in a fire in 1729. But we know from drawings and copies what it looked like, and can speculate on Grünewald's opinions of it. It represented the *Coronation of the Virgin* and was a monumental symmetrical composition, as fully of the High Renaissance as Titian's *Assumption of the Virgin* of ten years later. There were two zones, one of the Earth, the other of the Heavens. The apostles were mighty figures in ample mantles, yet drawn with infinite care for details such as hair and wrinkles. Above, the Virgin knelt frontally and was crowned by God the Father and Christ seated to the left and right. The middle axis was finally restated at the top of the picture by the lower part of a circular halo of red, orange and yellow tones in which, just above the crown of the Virgin, appeared the Dove, symbol of the Holy Spirit.

Dürer's Heller Altarpiece has been described, because Grünewald knew it and contributed to it in a very different spirit. That spirit, the spirit of Grünewald's art, is what must now engage our attention.

IV

It speaks eloquently in his paintings, eloquently enough for reproductions to convey the passionate urgency of its message. Yet both the message and the compositions of Grünewald's works are in need of more than what the immediate impact can give. A close analysis of at least some of the pictures illustrated in this book may be a help to uninitiated readers, even if no doubt unnecessary for those used to looking at the art of the North in its state between Gothic and Renaissance. The pictures chosen for the purpose are three from the Isenheim Altarpiece.

The *Crucifixion* (Plates 75–83) is a symmetrical composition, so calm and balanced that what the painting relates and how it is related comes as a reinforced shock. Christ hanging from the Cross is in the middle, to our left are the Virgin held by St John the Evangelist, and the kneeling Magdalene, to our right are St John the Baptist and the Lamb with Chalice and Cross. It is a strange choice of figures, iconographically unusual because St John the Baptist was dead at the time of the Crucifixion, and because a lamb with cross and chalice represents Christ's sacrifice on the Cross and should stand in its stead not by its side. The programme was suggested probably by the wish of Guido Guersi, the Sicilian preceptor of the Antonite house at Isenheim. The Antonites looked after those suffering from gangrene, epilepsy and that recent scourge, syphilis. When a sufferer was brought in, he was first led to the altar and prayers for miraculous healing were said. It is in the light of these pathetic and repulsive scenes that this *Crucifixion* must be seen.

The Cross is a raw piece knocked together roughly and without care. The body of Christ is big and strong, his head large and heavy. Blood pours down his face from the hideously long thorns of the Crown of Thorns, and his body is a greenish-grey, covered with weals and bruises. Horror could not be painted more ruthlessly. To look long at the figure is almost unbearable, though the sick at Isenheim may well have derived comfort from it. The loin-cloth is as rough as the wood of the Cross, and torn as if lacerated in the tortures or perhaps from the beginning chosen to be of no further value. Grünewald was strangely fond of imperfect, torn, ruined materials. Christ's feet are in a cramp, and the blood has run down them from the nail. His hands are forced by the nails into almost grotesque contortions of the fingers. They are outlined against a black night sky which is hardly set off against the dark brownish-greenish landscape below. Yet the widening river of green traversing the Cross at the height of Christ's knees binds together the groups on the left and right.

St John the Baptist is a strong figure too, his legs apart, his mantle a warm healthy red, his hand pointing to Christ. The meaning of the gesture is made patent by an inscription in gilt letters: "Illum oportet crescere me autem minui." It is a medieval trait to allow such *tituli* entry into a painted scene. Medieval also is the excessive length of the pointing finger. For the Middle Ages were ready to neglect true relations of size in favour of relations dictated by significance. X-rays have proved that only during work on the panel did Grünewald lengthen the finger. Christ's head also was not at first hanging so low and the body of the Magdalene was erect and not as it is now. Grünewald intensified as he went on.

The broad figure of St John the Baptist is balanced by the group of St John the Evangelist and the Virgin. There is faith in victory in the Baptist and heroism in extreme suffering in Christ, but the suffering of the others is passive. They are both frail. St John's body is extremely slender and hardly visible under the loose red mantle. His head is small, and the features as if they were melting. There is no emphasis on the bone structure. The mouth is small, loose and drooping at the corners, the eyes too are small and drooping at the corners. Even the hand supporting the Virgin seems to have no bones. The Virgin has fainted. The upper part of her body, above the waist, falls back as if felled. She is clothed in white, an iconographical anomaly of the first order. But white was needed here as a carrier of expression, and Grünewald—that is becoming more and more evident—does all he does for the sake of the intensity of expression.

14

The face of the Virgin is similar to that of St John, and that of the Magdalene is like a younger sister's. Yet the Magdalene's grief is a different grief, as her character is different. She wrings her small hands, hands as expressive as the Baptist's and set against a lighter patch in the dark greens of the landscape. And as she wrings her hands the whole of her arms are wrung, the sleeves forming tight, knotty coils. A transparent veil lies over her head and shoulders, sign of an elegance which distinguishes her and which is as eloquent in her silky, lustrous fair hair and the salmon-pink of her wide rippling dress.

These ripples and silky flows recur often in Grünewald's figures of women. They must have been expressive of his ideal of female beauty. An extreme case is the drawing of St Dorothy (Plate 33) with the ample mantle, closely pleated all over; another is the St Lucy (?) from the Heller Altarpiece (Plates 49, 51), an earlier and a little more conventional figure, but also with the mantle pleated like the fins on the underside of fungi, and a coquettish face—the only such worldly expression anywhere in Grünewald's *œuvre*. The puckered flesh of the face, the fingers rounded almost like sausages—nowhere is the firm body structure which gives permanence stressed in the way Dürer always stressed it from the moment he reached maturity.

Above the St Lucy in the Heller Altarpiece stood St Cyriacus exorcizing an evil spirit from the kneeling princess (Plates 53, 55, 56, 58). The same motifs and the same purposes need not be pointed out. The exorcizing is done by the saintly deacon pressing a thumb against the chin of the princess with such violence that the thumb is all bent, and at the same time by his pulling her kerchief in the opposite direction with such violence that her head is broken back like the upper part of the body of the Virgin in the *Crucifixion*. The princess's fingers can only be compared in expressiveness with those of Christ on the Cross, even if they express not death in extreme pain but the pain of a crisis, almost an orgasm. All forms are twisted and turned as in the Magdalene, but a comparison reveals how wide was the range of extreme expression at Grünewald's command.

The Magdalene and the group of the Virgin and St John are united in grief yet contrasted in character, and hence in expression of grief. But compositionally they form a group of closed triangular outline to balance the figure of the Baptist. Together they are broader, and that was needed, because the whole picture, contrary to what was stated at the beginning of this description, is not symmetrical. The Cross is not in the middle axis, but somewhat to the right. The fact remains disturbing, because one feels that Grünewald's intention here was a monumental, a Renaissance composition like Dürer's. The displacement has a purely technical, not a compositional, reason. The panel on which the *Crucifixion* is painted consists of two separate halves, and Christ on the Cross could not be painted so that the dividing line ran right down his body. The division of the panels was a necessity, because the altarpiece has movable wings, and behind the *Crucifixion* lay another scene to be revealed on other occasions.

V

This scene is really two scenes separated by a division enabling this second stage of the altarpiece again to open and reveal a third (Plates 89–102). The scene is usually called *Christmas* or the *Nativity*, but the concert of angels on the left is not part of it: what one calls the *Nativity* is a group comprising the seated Virgin and Child in a light green hilly landscape with distant grey-blue mountains. Nearer her is the gateway of the *hortus conclusus* in which she sits, the rose-bush which belongs to her iconographically and a big blackish-green bush on the left which leads the eye to the other half of the picture. She is clothed in the traditional warm red with the traditional dark blue mantle. Her hair is like gold, her face so suffused by light that the mouth and eyes float in the almost unmodulated surface. Her hands, hands again with fingers bent as if they had no bones, hold the baby high up. His little fingers, fingers much like those of his mother, play with a rosary. The napkin is torn, a sign of humility or a deliberate, violent reminder of the loin-cloth of the *Crucifixion*. Otherwise there are no forebodings of the Passion. If the *Crucifixion* had expressed the excess of pain, here is the excess of bliss, a bliss poured over the young mother in streams of light from on high. God the Father is hardly visible in an aureole of yellow. White hair and white beard and a Gothic glory can only be guessed. And then the light streams down, yellow, turning a vapoury mauvy-pink as it passes dark greyish-blue clouds and greyish-blue crags. Angels disport themselves in it, more of them than one realizes at first. In the end, before the cascade reaches the yellow halo of the Virgin, we know no longer whether we see light transformed or deep gullies in the mountain-side.

Beside the Virgin on the ground stands a low little bed, the simple bath trough with a towel, and a glass bottle or carafe to feed the baby with. The trough stands in front of, the bottle on the steps of, the curious pavilion which fills the left part of the painting. It is a structure in the Gothic style and represents its last and most fantastic phase. Dürer, about 1512–15, would have introduced the Italian fashion. Grüne-wald takes notice of this only later in the Snow Altarpiece of 1517–19 (Plates 123–30) and the scene at Karlsruhe of *Christ carrying the Cross* (Plates 140–2). Grünewald's Gothic forms are those of the most inventive architects and carvers of those years: nodding ogee arches, extremely attenuated shafts with twisted bases, curly and frilly crockets and sudden sprays of completely naturalistic foliage. It is the style of the St Laurence Portal at Strassburg but even more of Benedict Rieth in Prague and his Saxon followers of about 1520.

The introduction of these tendrils and leaves is significant. Are they painted to represent what is real or are they painted to represent what is carved with a view to look real? Layers of possibilities are superimposed on the plain, easy, unambiguous truth. On one of the wings of the *Crucifixion* St Sebastian appears, as real with his scarlet mantle as the Baptist in the *Crucifixion*, yet evidently meant to be a statue

(Plates 70–72); for he stands on an intricate plinth, decorated with a naturalistic spray of foliage coloured stone grey to represent carved stone. The column behind St Sebastian has instead of a capital another such spray, much ampler, indeed for a capital as excessive as the thorns were of the Crown of Thorns. What is the function of those ambiguous displays? One function Grünewald has in common with the carvers who carved them. They wanted neither the structural logic of base and capital nor their static security. They wanted growth instead, and the nature-made form rather than the man-made.

The whole pavilion, indeed, is hardly acceptable as man-made. Admittedly the Alsace builds in red sandstone, but the red here is as fire or as malachite, the colour of a fabulous vision rather than a building. In it and in front of it angels make music. The three most prominent ones play viols. The most delightful is the child at the front, in her pale pink dress and with her light fair hair. She has a chubby face and small pink wings, and her plump hands are all contorted with the intense abandon of her mood. Behind her are two stranger things, one a feathered seraph all greenish-brown and looking at first as though covered with an artichoke growth of leaves, the other one fiery red and in front of a fiery red aura in which a baby angel appears. Another angel is in a green aura and many more, yellow, red, blue and green, have turned up for this concert. But the concert is not the accompaniment of the Virgin on the other side of the picture. It refers to a much smaller second apparition of the Virgin, kneeling in profile in the pavilion and raising her hands in prayer. Her halo is of such intensity that her face and body are absorbed by it. The eye sees no more than a dazzle of red and golden light and in their centre a white face, and red lips, two red eyes and a red crown. The body is transfigured in light as had been the longing of the great mystics. The source of this strange image is indeed a vision, the Revelations of St Bridget, a fourteenth-century Swedish nun. They had been printed in Germany in 1500 and 1502 (the latter edition in German), and there, in the last section *De Excellentia B. M. Virginis*, we read of the body of the child Virgin like a crystal vessel, like a radiant light, like a flame, and of the love of the angels for the child Virgin.

This painting of *Christmas* and the *Angel Concert* has no centre in the sense of the Renaissance and the *Crucifixion*. Its focal-points are the pale yellow glory of God and the fiery glory of the praying Virgin, two states of supernatural light, set off by the earthly happiness of the bigger and more solid figure of the Virgin on the right. But balance is to a certain extent restored by the wings. They correspond to one another compositionally, if not in substance: the *Annunciation* on the left in a Gothic setting with a central arch into the chapel-like interior (Plates 84–88), and the *Resurrection* on the right with the most wonderful of Grünewald's haloes (Plates 103–6). Here Christ rises from the grave and the world of the armed men falling higgledy-piggledy to the ground, rises along the bluish-white shroud which turns mauve and darker mauve and so to the flaming and overwhelming yellow it assumes under the reflections of the aureole. This has a yellow centre merging into a gentle red and finally a soothing pale green merging with the dark night sky. Christ's head, like that of the little praying Virgin, is transformed. There is no bone left, nor any flesh. It is a vision of majesty and bliss unsurpassed anywhere at any time.

VI

During precisely the years of the Isenheim Altarpiece, most probably in 1513, Raphael painted the *Sistine Madonna*. They represent the extreme possibilities of that moment of high blessing in European art—one static, the other dynamic; one final, the other always seemingly changing its state; one primarily expressing itself in form, the other in light and colour. And yet the same style can be recognized in both. For the *Resurrection* also is a Renaissance composition in that it is central and frontal like the *Sistine Madonna*. And even the whole composition of *Nativity*, *Angel Concert*, *Annunciation* and *Resurrection* is, as has been said, symmetrical, though as the result of a more complex process of balancing. The three heavenly emanations of light are placed at the points of a triangle which interlocks with an earthly triangle of Virgin and Child, arches of the pavilion and group of the *Annunciation*.

The two halves of the panel with the *Nativity* and the *Angel Concert* can be thrown open as could be those of the *Crucifixion*, and behind them appear three carved statues, the work of ten years earlier. Nicholas of Hagenau, the carver, possessed some of the intensity that drove Grünewald, but about 1500 its vehicle was still the splintering line. To make light its vehicle was Grünewald's achievement, as it was in Italy at the same time—with fuller sensuality and lesser intensity—Giorgione's and Titian's.

In his mastery of celestial light lies Grünewald's European and *a fortiori* his German contribution. As a painter he towers above Dürer, even if, as universal human achievement, his work cannot be compared with Dürer's. A comparison between the iris on Grünewald's *Virgin of Stuppach* (Plates 126–30) and that on Dürer's Virgin in the National Gallery is proof of that. But Grünewald's superiority over Dürer does not extend to the relentless intensity which we have seen at work in his paintings. For Dürer, in certain drawings such as the Death on a mare of 1505 and the portrait of his mother of 1514, showed that within his immense range of possibilities that possibility also existed. However, he did not want it to dominate, to eclipse other emotional or intellectual tasks. Hence, of his woodcuts and engravings of the *Crucifixion* and the *Mourning of the Dead Christ* none are as poignant as Grünewald's.

Dürer was a man of wide-ranging possibilities, Grünewald's was a single mind; Dürer explored many techniques, even that of etching on iron plates, Grünewald only painted and drew; Dürer's subject-matter covers the genre-scene and the antique allegory, the textbook illustration and the ornamental pattern, landscape and the nude; Grünewald is exclusively a religious painter. Dürer's genius can only be assessed by exploring the whole of his *œuvre*; Grünewald is to a rare degree a one-work artist. Know the Isenheim Altarpiece, and you know his genius. Out of eleven other certain works of his, three are variations on the themes of the Isenheim *Crucifixion*, one paraphrases the Isenheim *Lamentation*, one the Isenheim Virgin of the Nativity. Dürer was watchful of himself, he recorded what happened to him, provided it with dates and comments, tried to see himself as history; Grünewald for all we can guess was silent about himself, less articulate probably, and less in the public eye too (although, for example, Melanchthon knew him and mentioned him in 1531 side by side with Dürer and Cranach). Dürer's was indeed a long, consistent development; Grünewald appears amazingly "complete" in his first certain picture, the *Mocking of Christ* of 1503 (Plates 43, 44).

Dürer's final ideal was repose, though without loss of intensity. In his *Four Apostles* of 1526 and the late drawings of the Virgin with saints he achieved it by undergoing and transforming the experience of the Italian Renaissance. Grünewald's ideal, in spite of the Renaissance or Dürer's influence on his compositions, remained the Gothic ideal of the maximum intensity within the appropriate mood. Or is this not a Gothic ideal upheld but a Baroque ideal anticipated, as Correggio in Italy was anticipating it in the same years? It is useless to look for an answer, just as useless as it is to argue whether Dürer ought to be kept in the Gothic or the Renaissance drawer.

The polarity between Dürer and Grünewald remains. It is an eminently German polarity, present again when German literature culminated. Goethe belonged to "*Sturm und Drang*" when he wrote his panegyric on Strassburg Cathedral and his *Götz von Berlichingen*, he was a romantic when he had the vision of the last scene of the second part of *Faust*, but he was a classic in his *Iphigenie* and a classic in his ideal of discipline and perfect form. His was a long development, a development which he watched and commented on. Novalis, Hölderlin, Kleist were on the side of the opposition, of the incomplete, the ever growing, the blue flower and the transfusing light.

But Dürer's and Goethe's mature works were the success of self-educative efforts; Dürer's *Apocalypse*, and Goethe's *Erwin von Steinbach* were natural. Hence classic moments are rare in Germany, romantic schools and periods frequent, from Meister Eckart about 1300 to the Baroque lyrics and finally to Expressionism. Nothing could be more characteristic than the fact that Germany has hardly any rationally ordered abstract art, and France hardly any Expressionism (though Cézanne was French, van Gogh was not). And nothing could be more characteristic than the fact that Grünewald was first comprehensively presented in 1911 and first revealed to the German public in two books of 1919, one by an art historian whose speciality was the Spanish Baroque, the other by one whose passion was Händel's operas.

THE ARTIST AND HIS WORKS

by Michael Meier

In compiling the notes on the artist and his works that follow, I have drawn upon the entire field of Grünewald study. I am particularly indebted to Heinrich Alfred Schmid and Walter Karl Zülch, whose findings were published in 1911 and 1938 respectively, but also to all those who have drawn attention to hitherto unknown works or important new sources and have thus helped to establish a picture of the artist and his work.

Parts of the notes on the paintings from the first edition of Lorenz Dittmann's study on Grünewald's use of colour (Werner R. Deusch, 1939) have been incorporated in this volume. The catalogue and the notes on the drawings represent a certain amount of gentle sifting of the numerous attempts at interpretation, to allow an unprejudiced approach—if indeed this is at all possible—and perhaps to open up further discussion.

Mathis Gothardt Neithardt

The creator of the Isenheim Altarpiece, whom his first biographer, Joachim von Sandrart (1606–88) called Grünewald, was known to his contemporaries as Mathis the Painter, Mathis von Seligenstadt, von Würzburg, or, as Dürer called him, simply Mathes. He called himself Mathis Gothart and also Mathis Nithart. An inventory of his estate refers to "Meister Mathis Nithart oder Gothart" ("Master Mathis Nithart or Gothart") and thus gives no indication of the actual surname or the sequence in which the two names were used. The very few signed examples of Mathis's work show a G within an M; in two cases (of which only one is clearly established) an N has been added: Mathis Gothar(d)t N(e)ithar(d)t.

Very little is known about the artist as a man. For there are so far no documents with comments by Mathis. Only a sketch in Oxford bears his short, mutilated signature. No self-portrait exists (in contrast to Dürer, Cranach and Hans Baldung), unless we are willing to see Mathis's features in the strong, yet gentle, face of St Sebastian at Isenheim.

Thus everything known about Grünewald, his real name, his social background and other details about his personal life, has been discovered recently as the result of painstaking research. But it has little bearing on his work. For the very paintings mentioned in documents have disappeared, and there are few references to any in existence.

Mathis was born in Würzburg, probably between 1475 and 1480. A prior date is unlikely, since the earliest painting attributable to him beyond doubt—the *Mocking of Christ*, in Munich—is an early work and not the product of a master at the height of his powers. He is, then, younger than Dürer and Cranach and most definitely younger than Hans Holbein the Elder, to whom his work seems to be fundamentally indebted. Although it is not known where Mathis was apprenticed and where he travelled, an early theory, based on the study of his colour, has gained ground recently. It suggests that he may have known the elder Holbein and had perhaps worked under him in Augsburg.

From 1501 until 1525 his name appears in the rate-books of Seligenstadt, a small town on the river Main, with a charter of its own, three hours' walk down-river from Aschaffenburg, where he possessed a house and probably ran a workshop. Hans Memling was born there sixty years earlier. Mathis, though he appears to have retained his original abode, became court painter and adviser on matters of art to the archbishop of Mainz, Uriel von Gemmingen, who was in residence at Aschaffenburg. He was given a coat of arms, in view of his position, and administered funds for his master. These were used for rebuilding the castle at Aschaffenburg to Mathis's designs, which included a chimney-piece, whose execution was entrusted to a Frankfurt stone-mason (1511). Disputes about payment later led to a protracted court case in Frankfurt am Main. Although it lasted for one and a half years (1514–15), the parties involved did not manage to get "Master Mathis, the painter, who designed or commissioned the work, at the time servant of myself (the defendant) archbishop of Mainz", to appear in court. The documents of the case provide most of present-day knowledge about the master's life. They are evidence of Mathis's versatility as painter, designer and superintendent of the castle's reconstruction. They also reveal that he painted a panel for the Frankfurt Dominicans in their monastery in 1511, where attempts were made to arrest him in connexion with demands for payment.

But the master must have worked in the church of the Dominicans before that date. Sandrart saw a *Transfiguration* there—perhaps the work mentioned above—and the wings of the Heller Altarpiece (1509), now happily completed by recent finds, came from this church. Thus Mathis was also working for other clients during his employment at the archiepiscopal court. Indeed, this had happened before and was to be repeated later, as his surviving works (the Basle *Crucifixion*, the one in Washington, the Munich *Mocking of Christ* and the Isenheim Altarpiece) testify.

Besides the archbishop of Mainz, two prominent clerics affected Mathis's art profoundly: Guido Guersi, preceptor of the Antonites at Isenheim, and Heinrich Reitzmann, an Aschaffenburg prelate. Commissions from both seem to have come at the same time, and it appears that Mathis delayed work on the altarpiece for Oberissigheim—if it was indeed executed at all—for the sake of the bigger undertaking at Isenheim. Work on a further commission for the last-named patron—the Altarpiece of the Virgin of the Snow, already ordered in 1513—was not begun until 1517, since Isenheim obviously required the master's fullest attention.

The Order of St Anthony, whose parent abbey was in the Dauphiné, enjoyed a great reputation for the care of the sick. It maintained a large monastery in the little town of Isenheim in southern Alsace. Most of the preceptors were Italian or French, such as Jean d'Orliac, who had held this office since 1475. His portrait appears on a triptych by the Colmar master Martin Schongauer (now in the Unterlindenmuseum, Colmar, and formerly in the rood-loft of the Order's church). Orliac had himself painted as a donor on another occasion: for the shrine of the high altar of his church, with wings to be added by Mathis. At that time Orliac had been in retirement for a considerable period (since 1490), so that the completion of the high altar had become the responsibility of his successor, Guido Guersi. It is not known what caused him to entrust Mathis the Painter with this important task. Perhaps Mathis already had connexions with other branches of the Antonite Order or it may be that his reputation at that time had already reached Isenheim. Whatever the assumption, it seems strange that Guersi, an Italian, should have caused a German artist to create one of the greatest works of art in existence today. It is all the more remarkable since—on the basis of available information—Mathis had never, apart from his last years, been active beyond the narrow confines of his native province. It is not known how far the master's work was affected by Guersi. But it may be assumed that he was not without influence on the choice and representation of the subject. The work was already finished at the time of his death in 1516 and includes him as a monastic saint in a disputation—an old man with a distinguished head, who also appears in one of Mathis's sketches.

Meanwhile Heinrich Reitzmann had repeatedly pressed his order for the Altarpiece of the Virgin of the Snow. The chapel in the Aschaffenburg collegiate church, for which this work had been intended, had already been consecrated in 1516. In 1517, the preparation of the necessary colours is discussed, while 1519 is inscribed on the shrine as the date of completion. The shrine alone has remained in its original place, for the wings were soon dispersed (Freiburg im Breisgau, Stuppach). In addition, Mathis is said to have been summoned to Aschaffenburg (1517), because the city fathers wanted his views about a fountain.

In 1516 Mathis was again employed in Aschaffenburg, this time by Albrecht von Brandenburg, who had ruled since 1514 as archbishop-elector and was made a cardinal in 1518. As a courtier Mathis wore costly robes, velvet, furs and gold jewellery, had a regular income and also accompanied his master on his travels. On a visit to Aachen for the emperor's coronation in 1520 he met Albrecht Dürer, who wrote that he gave "Mathes" examples of his work to the value of two florins, perhaps not without the hope that Mathis might recommend him to Albrecht. It is the only record of a meeting between the two artists and indeed of Mathis having had contact with any other great contemporary master. There would have been ample opportunity for such contacts at the art- and splendour-loving court of the humanist Albrecht, who was painted by Cranach, and whose portrait was engraved by Dürer on copper. The archiepiscopal see of Mainz had been the centre of the great spiritual unrest of the period. Luther, moved by Albrecht's trade in indulgences, having published his theses and conducted a fearless, deliberately provoking correspondence with the archbishop, thus setting the stage for the Reformation. Germany at that time resounded with the predictions of old and new prophets, with the rumblings of fanatics and dreamers. There was ferment amongst the poorer sections of society, great events which were also to affect the life of Mathis cast their shadow.

It appears that the artist did not take a personal part in these upheavals. Around 1520 he painted three altarpieces—which have since vanished—for chapels in Mainz Cathedral, and, by order of the archbishop, a great panel (now in Munich) destined for the altar of St Maurice in the collegiate church at Halle. It shows a meeting between the two saints, Erasmus and Maurice, and in its restrained splendour is evidence of the artist having been at his most mature. His last surviving works are the altarpiece at Tauberbischofsheim, whose donor and original site are unknown, and a *Lamentation*, now in Aschaffenburg. Both probably date from 1525.

The Peasants' War broke out in that year and caused great changes in the region of the Middle Rhine and in Franconia, Mathis's native province and the scene of his activity. The riots shook all Germany and also gained ground in Halle, where Cardinal Albrecht was only saved from violence by the court chaplain, Winkler, who had Lutheran sympathies. In 1526 the cardinal was able to return to Aschaffenburg, where the rebels had forced his representative to capitulate, and held reckoning. All participants in the rising were severely punished, all suspected of Lutheranism dismissed from service at court, the guilds were deprived of their ancient privileges and the town of Seligenstadt lost its charter. It is probable that Mathis also lost his position at that time. In 1526 he received once more a sum from the exchequer, but it was to be his last. After apprenticing his adopted son Andreas with a woodcarver —the only known item of his family life—he left his home and moved to Frankfurt am Main, where he made his will. He probably chose the free Imperial city because it offered him some safety, and lodged there with the silk embroiderer, Hans von Saarbrücken. He also seems to have worked as a soap-maker, had a court case over some money he had lent, and received a commission from Magdeburg to draw the mills on the Main, so that similar mills could be built at Magdeburg from his drawings.

When he moved to Halle at a later, unknown, date, he left a great many of his possessions with Hans von Saarbrücken. Mathis lived in the houses of various friends at Halle. The Bible of one of these friends, Hans Plock, a silk embroiderer, was discovered recently, with several sketches from Mathis's hand. There is no indication as to what he did in Halle. A report only mentions that he was supposed to have taken charge of the municipal waterworks. But he had "unfortunately not achieved a great deal", when he died in August 1528. Those present at his death were entrusted with the care of his adopted son, who was to inherit the master's entire property in Halle and Frankfurt. The authorities in Frankfurt compiled shortly afterwards a catalogue of his possessions—an extensive list of valuable clothes, painter's equipment, colours, jewellery, technical literature (on mining); also Lutheran writings and two paintings, one showing the crucified Christ between the Virgin and St John. His works were very much in demand after his death, as sixteenth-century literature and attempts at purchases by various seventeenth-century princes show. The man himself was quickly forgotten, confused with others and eventually, through Sandrart, came to be known as Grünewald. The Isenheim Altarpiece was thought to be by Dürer until the nineteenth century; other works were attributed to Hans Baldung or vice versa, so that Mathis the artist, too, while not exactly forgotten, soon became a legendary figure.

This obscurity, attached to the man and his work, is not entirely fortuitous. It is purely accidental that much information about Mathis was lost. At the same time, the meagre information contained in documents could hardly explain his art: a court painter with a fixed salary, leading a respectable existence, has created the concert of angels in the *Christmas* picture and the wonderful *Resurrection*, bathed in light. He has endowed the traditional representation of the Crucifixion with a power unknown before or since. The glow of his colours was unsurpassed at the time, the fantastic visions in his paintings of the Virgin are—even with some knowledge of their literary sources—unique as works of art. The master might be thought to have been under the immediate impact of a sudden inspiration, but closer examination shows that the numerous improvements are the product of conscientious effort and of the highest standards of craftsmanship. The concept of an entire altarpiece, the details of the composition, the harmony or discordance of the colours are revealed as the results of the most exact calculation, as a new instrument, invented by Mathis to enable him to carry out his intentions. The critical observer is apt to split what is a living organism into its components, though it can only be experienced as a whole. For "the needs governing the creations of a genius are less apparent than the arbitrariness in the work of the moderately gifted" (M. J. Friedländer). And it is unlikely that we shall ever find the uniqueness of his genius reflected in sixteenth-century documents.

Commentary on the Drawings

Tradition reports far more drawings from the hand of Mathis Gothardt Neithardt than we know today. Joachim von Sandrart saw an album of Mathis's chalk drawings in the house of the Frankfurt painter Philipp Uffenbach. The same album is mentioned by the French diplomat B. de Monconys (1663–4). At that time the collection was already owned by Abraham Schelkens of Frankfurt. No one knows its eventual fate. But it can be assumed that it originally contained the drawings found by M. J. Friedländer in the Savigny Collection. An inventory of the Amerbach Kunstkabinett in Basle (1586) lists twenty drawings by "Mathis von Aschenburg", of which none have been traced so far. The collection of the Strassburg alderman B. C. Künast (1589–1667) contained amongst its 723 "objects" some works of "Matheus Grien". Eleven of Mathis's drawings from the collection of the Leipzig senator Gottfried Winckler were auctioned in 1815. Five of these (Plates 6, 15/17, 16/18) were later discovered in public collections, but there appears to be no trace of the rest. It is therefore quite probable that still more will eventually turn up, like the three leaves (Plates 2–4) found in a Bible in the Märkisches Museum, Berlin. Style and origin may suggest that they are original drawings by Mathis. But the genuineness of six drawings discovered in 1950 near Marburg is still rightly disputed. Although students have been denied access to the originals, published reproductions suggest that they are not from Mathis's hand, though they might be in a similar manner. They are therefore neither illustrated nor described in this volume, where only the established group of thirty-eight studies and one not yet generally acknowledged sketch for a complete painting have been listed and reproduced in full.

Mathis's works, so small in quantity and of such great artistic value, suffered during the recent war. All the studies from the Dresden Print Room are missing (Plates 6, 8, 15/17), as is the large sheet from Lützschena (Plates 11/12). A sheet from the East Berlin Print Room (Plates 16/18) is said to be in Moscow, the great nude trumpeter, formerly in the Koenigs Collection (Plate 22), was lost with the Dresden drawings. But there is hope that the loss of these irreplaceable works is not final.

Almost every one of Mathis's drawings has, like his paintings, been subject to the most varied and contradictory interpretations. Perhaps this is so because the master's works cannot be wholly interpreted. The drawings, in particular, have also defied all attempts at an exact chronological classification. A broad sequence has been established for the drawings, in which the Karlsruhe sketch of Christ on the Cross (Plate 1) can be set at the beginning, the drawing probably of the aged Margret Prellwitz (Plate 38) at the end. But anything in between can only be grouped in relation to individual known or reputed paintings and cannot be dated very accurately. This includes the group of studies linked with the lost Frankfurt *Transfiguration* (Plates 2–8) and everything showing some connexion with the Isenheim Altarpiece

(Plates 9–21; 1512–16), as well as some preliminary studies, probably for two of the three lost Mainz altarpieces and counting amongst his finest works (Plates 29–34; 1520). The sketch of St John for the Tauberbischofsheim *Crucifixion* is a later work. Everything else—such as the Oxford drawing and the portrait study in the Louvre, or the head of the stout man in Stockholm—could at best be dated only very arbitrarily. The four drawings (Plates 12–14, 19), which ostensibly depict a woman at different stages of her life, have been dated according to the subject's assumed age, and therefore would have been begun in 1503 and finished in 1523. But stylistic criteria do not confirm this view and point to a very much shorter interval between them. The stout man (Plate 37) belongs to a type which already appears on the wings of the earlier Lindenhardt Altarpiece (right-hand panel, St Egidius). It bears a strong resemblance to the face of Rudolf von Scherenberg, bishop of Würzburg, whose monument of 1499 is a work of Tilman Riemenschneider. Nevertheless, on stylistic grounds it should be placed with the later works. Another late drawing, the so-called "Trias Romana" (Plate 35) shows the right profile of a man who apparently had also served as a model for the Frankfurt *Transfiguration* (Plate 8). We can therefore assume that similar types in drawings many years apart were either models used by Mathis throughout his life or simply a characteristic feature of his style.

The themes of his drawings are even more difficult to assess than their sequence. This is understandable in the case of preliminary sketches for paintings now lost. But surviving works prove that Mathis never rigidly stuck to his drawings and always made considerable changes, indeed often only partly used his sketches. The drawings are almost without exception studies; that is to say, they enabled certain objects, the human form, attitudes, or draperies to be examined in detail and recorded. "Unfinished studies", as some of his drawings are dubbed, do not exist. All are equally perfect and highly finished—even the delicate forms on Plates 23 and 31, which are studies in the distribution of light and shade. Mathis enriches alert and careful observation with an extraordinarily strong imagination in which fantasy and sobriety are combined, as for example in the glorious St Dorothy (Plate 33), where an astrolabe—which probably lay in the workshop near the model entirely by accident—is shown next to the figure of the saint. Screen and platform, both ordinary workshop equipment, also appear in the painting, without suggesting more than a purely fortuitous presence. The delightful study of the cloak (Plate 25) shows again platform and astrolabe. But what is the function of the branches that stem the heavy flow of the train? It would be quite futile to assign an exact meaning to this fantastic medley. Although there has hitherto been a reluctance to mention workshop equipment and models in connexion with Mathis, it seems necessary when looking at his work to accept their existence. The powerful drawing of St John for the Tauberbischofsheim panel (Plate 36) is based on the living model. The model was a young man with unkempt beard and moustache, curly hair and a very ugly nose. Comparison with the head of St John in the painting shows that the features of the model have disappeared in the finished work, so that—apart from a very general likeness—only an expression of sorrow in the features and in the bearing of head and hands have been transferred. The drawings for the Frankfurt *Transfiguration* are mainly studies of movement and drapery. Clearly recognizable amongst the figures (Plates 6–8) is the smooth floor of the workshop. The portrait drawings already mentioned are also studies made to examine the expressiveness of different movements of head and hands. For example, the woman in the Lützschena drawing (Plate 11) folds her hands over some object, possibly a book, to give them support and the desired pose.

If we consider the drawings in the light of these assumptions, it seems quite likely that the head of the screaming man (Plate 30) is a preliminary study for the saint in the *Temptation of St Anthony*. There was no need for the model to provide in detail the features of the figure in the actual painting, since Plate 30 is a representation of a man crying out and throwing back his tortured head rather than of hagiographic items with which the master was in any case familiar. The strangely puffed sleeve in a Berlin drapery study (Plate 3) may also be explained by a garment worn by the model.

One might be tempted, on the strength of this, to see in Mathis more than a late Gothic painter, or—perhaps in contrast to Dürer—the last great artist of the Middle Ages. For his drawings are unconventional and bear little of the stamp of tradition. They show, on the contrary, so much observation and active study, that their creator must be considered a true man of his time, an artist of the dawning sixteenth century. It is the age which numbers among its great men Leonardo, to whose sketches and method Mathis's drawings show considerable kinship, as others have already pointed out.

Our catalogue is based on these assumptions. It therefore gives a very detailed and sometimes perhaps rather involved description of the drawings to avoid suggesting subjects they do not, in fact, represent. No attempts at dating and interpretation have been made beyond the broadly outlined possibilities.

BIBLIOGRAPHY

Only the most important books and articles are listed.

GENERAL:

Schmid, H. A. *Die Gemälde und Zeichnungen von Mathias Grünewald*, Vol. 1 plates; Vol. 2 text, Strassburg, 1908 and 1911.

Feurstein, H. "Zur Deutung des Bildgehalts bei Grünewald", *Beiträge zur Geschichte der Deutschen Kunst*, Augsburg, 1924.

Fraenger, W. *Matthias Grünewald, ein physiognomischer Versuch*, Berlin, 1936.

Zülch, W. K. *Der historische Grünewald, Mathis Gothardt Neithardt*, Munich, 1938.

Burkhard, A. *Mathias Grünewald, Personality and Accomplishment*, Cambridge, 1936.

Vogt, A. M. *Grünewald, Meister gegenklassischer Malerei*, Zürich, 1957.

GRÜNEWALD'S USE OF COLOUR:

Dittmann, L. *Die Farbe bei Grünewald*, Munich, 1955.

THE DONAUESCHINGEN PANELS:

Salm, C. Count. *Münchner Jahrbuch*, Vol. 2, pp. 118 ff., 1951.

THE DRAWINGS:

FACSIMILE EDITIONS:

Meder, J. *Albertina Faksimile*, Vienna, 1920.

Storck, W. F. "Handzeichnungen Grünewalds", *1. Druck der Gesellschaft für zeichnende Künste*, Munich, 1922.

Friedländer, M. J. *Die Grünewaldzeichnungen der Sammlung von Savigny*, Berlin, 1926.

CRITICAL STUDIES:

Schoenberger, G. *The drawings of Mathis Gothart Nithart called Grünewald*, New York, 1948.

Behling, L. *Die Handzeichnungen des Mathis Gothart Nithart genannt Grünewald*, Weimar, 1955.

THE NEWLY DISCOVERED BERLIN DRAWINGS:

Stengel, W. "Der neue Grünewaldfund", *Zeitschrift für Kuntswissenschaft*, Vol. 6, pp. 65 ff., Berlin, 1952.

THE STOCKHOLM SKETCH:

Schilling, E. "Eine Federzeichnung des 16. Jahrhunderts und ihre Beziehung zu Grünewald", *Städel-Jahrbuch*, Vol. 9, 1935.

THE MARBURG DISCOVERIES:

Dettweiler, F. "Die bei Marburg gefundenen Grünewaldzeichnungen", *Kunstchronik*, No. 3, Section 12, pp. 232 ff., 1950.

Zülch, W. K. "Die Marburger Grünewaldzeichnungen", *Aschaffenburger Jahrbuch*, Vol. 1, pp. 140 ff., 1952.

Winkler, F. "Der Marburger Grünewaldfund", *Zeitschrift für Kunstwissenschaft*, Vol. 6, pp. 155 ff., 1952.

Niemeyer, W. "Hans Grimmer, ein deutscher Manierist als Gewinn der Marburger Zeichnungsfunde", *Zeitschrift für Kunstgeschichte*, Vol. 16, No. 1, pp. 61 ff., 1953.

CATALOGUE

Drawings

1 Christ on the Cross

Kunsthalle, Karlsruhe

Chalk, heightened with white; 20⅞×12⅝ in., 53·1×32 cm.

Later cut out and stuck on. It was originally larger, as a copy at Basle (21⅝×15⅜ in., 55×39 cm.) shows. The left hand has been rubbed off, there are later repairs under the wrist and on the Cross itself, to the right above the horizontal beam. There is a later inscription from another hand: "Hohl Bain deli: (neavit) M P". The drawing was originally at Basle. About 1503.

2–4 Three studies which were found in 1952 partly cut out and stuck into a copy of Luther's translation of the Bible

The Bible was printed in 1541 by Lufft in Wittenberg, and belonged to the silk embroiderer Hans Plock, who had worked in Halle for Cardinal Albrecht and who was a friend of Mathis. It is possible that he took these drawings after Mathis's death. They belong to the same series as No. 5 and are generally considered preliminary studies for the last panel of a *Transfiguration* painted by Mathis in 1511 for the Dominican house in Frankfurt am Main. The measurements of the leaves are 13¾×8⅝ in., 35×22 cm.

2 A man standing with his cloak pulled over his head (Elijah?)

Print Room, East Berlin

Chalk, heightened with white, over grey watercolour; 9½×6¼ in., 24×16 cm. (proportions of the figure).

Later cut out and stuck on. The label was added in the sixteenth century. The verso of the sheet bears the arms of Hans Plock.

3 A bearded man with outstretched arms (Moses?)

Print Room, East Berlin

Chalk, heightened with white, over grey watercolour; 9½×6¼ in., 24×16 cm. (proportions of the figure).

Partly cut out (head and left arm), painted in dark olive near the feet. The tablets with the inscription were stuck over the right arm in the sixteenth century. The right hand is a later addition.

4 A man with a candlestick (St John the Evangelist?)

Print Room, East Berlin

Chalk, heightened with white, over grey watercolour; 9½×6¼ in., 24×16 cm. (proportions of the figure).

The candlestick and parts of the dress were later painted red; the tablets with the inscriptions are sixteenth-century additions. The verso of the sheet bears the arms of Hans Plock.

5 A kneeling figure pointing with his finger

Print Room, West Berlin

Chalk, heightened with white, over grey watercolour; 9¼×6½ in., 23·5×16·5 cm. (proportions of the figure).

Inscribed tablets, added in the sixteenth century, were removed some time ago. The sleeves were later overpainted with crimson watercolour. From the Lepell Collection.

6–8 Three studies probably for the lost Frankfurt *Transfiguration* (1511)

No. 6 has an old inscription, "Frankfurt", and No. 8 shows a faint indication of the clouds seen by Sandrart on the painting (see below). Nos. 6 and 8 also suggest the motive of the apostles overwhelmed by the appearance of the prophets and blinded by Christ's radiance. This missing work is thought to have influenced a fresco of 1555 by Jörg Rathgeb in the Carmelite house at Frankfurt am Main—of which only a drawing exists—as well as other works, such as a sketch by Peter Flötner at Erlangen and a stucco relief of 1618 at Butzbach (Hessen). Sandrart writes of the *Transfiguration*, "The Transfiguration on Mount Tabor in water-colours is one of his [Mathis's] finest works. It shows Moses and Elijah within a cloud and the kneeling apostles." (*Teutsche Akademie der Edlen Bau-, Bild- und Malerei-Künste*, Nurem-berg, 1675, III, 5, p. 236.)

6 **A falling apostle, back view**
Formerly Print Room, Dresden
Chalk, heightened with white; $5\frac{3}{4} \times 8\frac{1}{4}$ in., 14·6×20·8 cm.

The upper left-hand corner bears the inscription "Frankfurt" (sixteenth century). From the G. Winckler Collection, Leipzig.

7 **Drapery study**
Private collection in the United States
Chalk; $5\frac{1}{8} \times 7\frac{1}{8}$ in., 13×18 cm.

The bottom right-hand corner bears a later inscription: "A. Durer". From the Oppen-heim Collection, London; later in the LeRoy M. Backus Collection, Seattle, and auctioned with the rest of the collection by the Schaeffer Gallery, New York.

8 **A falling apostle, side view**
Formerly Print Room, Dresden
Chalk, heightened with white; $5\frac{7}{8} \times 10\frac{3}{8}$ in., 14·8×26·3 cm.

From the G. Winckler Collection, Leipzig.

9–21 **Thirteen studies showing close links with the panels of the Isenheim Altar-piece (1512–16)**
This is especially marked in Nos. 12, 13, 15, 16 and 18, which were partly used by Mathis for the panels of the altarpiece. The other drawings fit into this group stylistically and in choice of subject. They also include a woman's head (No. 19), unconnected with Isenheim.

9 **Study of the Virgin, with one hand raised, for an *Annunciation***
Print Room, West Berlin

Chalk, heightened with white, over grey water-colour; $8\frac{1}{8} \times 8\frac{1}{4}$ in., 20·7×21 cm.

On the same type of paper as No. 21. From the Savigny Collection.

10 **Portrait of an old man (Guido Guersi?)**
Schlossmuseum, Weimar
Chalk, heightened with white; $13\frac{3}{8} \times 10$ in., 34·1×25·3 cm.

The watermark of the paper, a coat of arms sur-mounted by an R and two lilies, occurs in Mainz between 1506 and 1516. From the Rochlitz Collection.

11 **A woman gazing upwards with hands folded in prayer**
Formerly Speck von Sternburg Collection, Lützschena
Chalk; $15\frac{1}{8} \times 11\frac{1}{8}$ in., 38·4×28·3 cm.

12 **A woman gazing upwards with clasped hands**
Formerly Speck von Sternburg Collection, Lützschena
Chalk; verso of No. 11.

Brown stains, with a large rust mark above the left thumb.

13 **A woman gazing upwards and wringing her hands**
Reinhart Collection, Winterthur
Chalk; $15\frac{7}{8}$–$16\frac{1}{4} \times 11\frac{5}{8}$–$11\frac{7}{8}$ in., 40·3–41·4× 29·7–30·2 cm.

From the Savigny Collection; later in the Licht Collection.

14 **A woman with a veil on her head**
Ashmolean Museum, Oxford
Chalk; $15 \times 9\frac{1}{2}$ in., 38×24 cm. (cut at the sides).
Signed "(M)athis" in chalk on the left; above inscribed "Matsia" by another hand. To the right a sixteenth-century (?) note, which trans-lated means "This has been painted by Mathis

von Ossenburg, painter to the Elector of Mentz (Mainz). He inscribed it 'Mathis' with his own hand." From the Douce Collection.

15 Study of the lower arm of St Sebastian

Formerly Print Room, Dresden

Chalk; $9\frac{3}{8} \times 7\frac{1}{2}$ in., 23·8×18·9 cm. (cut).

Originally on the same sheet as No. 16, later cut off. From the G. Winckler Collection, Leipzig.

16 Study of the upper arm of St Sebastian

Formerly Print Room, East Berlin

Chalk; $11 \times 7\frac{5}{8}$ in., 27·9×19·5 cm. (cut).

Nos. 15 and 16 form one study, which was used almost unchanged for the upper portion of the body of St Sebastian at Isenheim. The later inscription on the right of No. 16 reads "Wohlgemuth"; on the left is a collector's mark. From the G. Winckler Collection, Leipzig.

17 A seated old man

Formerly Print Room, Dresden

Chalk, heightened with white; verso of No. 15 (cut).

18 An old man seated under a tree

Formerly Print Room, East Berlin

Chalk, heightened with white; verso of No. 16 (cut).

In the upper right-hand corner an old inscription: "Isnaw" (Isenheim). Used by Mathis with only small changes for the figure of St Anthony on the panel with the two hermits.

19 A woman's head, front view

Louvre, Paris

Chalk; $7\frac{7}{8} \times 5\frac{3}{4}$ in., 20·1×14·7 cm.

In the upper left-hand corner a faked Dürer monogram. To the right of the centre and below the collector's marks of Robert de Cotte and Nicolas Coypel. Acquired from the Jabach Collection, Cologne, in 1671.

20 Portrait known as "Mathis's self-portrait"

Universitätsbibliothek, Erlangen

Originally chalk, heightened with white, later traced by another hand in pen and ink; $8\frac{1}{8} \times 6$ in., 20·6×15·2 cm.

On the left a monogram, G within M; above, the date 1529 (both later additions). Mathis used the drawing for the head of St Paul in the panel with two hermits. It was later used by Sandrart in the first edition of his *Teutschen Akademie* as a model for the portrait of Grünewald. A later copy of the same drawing (Cassel, early seventeenth century) is inscribed "Contrafactur des hochberümpten Maler Mathes von Aschaffenburg" ("Portrait of the famous painter Mathes von Aschaffenburg"). The names of twenty-five artists were inscribed on the back of the Erlangen drawing around 1600, with "Mathes von Aschaffenburg" listed fifth. Probably at one time in the possession of Dr Stromer, personal physician of Cardinal Albrecht of Brandenburg.

21 Study of the Virgin, with hands folded in prayer, for an *Annunciation*

Print Room, West Berlin

Chalk; $6\frac{1}{4} \times 5\frac{3}{4}$ in., 16×14·6 cm.

On the same type of paper as Nos. 9 and 34. Used by Mathis for the Isenheim *Annunciation* panel. From the Savigny Collection.

22 A nude man blowing a war-trumpet

Formerly Koenigs Collection, Haarlem

Chalk; $10\frac{5}{8} \times 7\frac{5}{8}$ in., 27·1×19·5 cm.

Right and left hand do not seem to finger the same instrument. From the Savigny Collection.

23 St Peter

Albertina, Vienna

Chalk, heightened with white; $14\frac{1}{2} \times 11\frac{5}{8}$ in., 36·8×29·6 cm.

Since the figure is obviously holding a large key, we feel justified in calling it a study of St Peter.

24 An old man standing with staff and sword

Albertina, Vienna

Chalk, heightened with white; verso of No. 23.

25 A kneeling figure in a wide cloak with two angels as train-bearers

Print Room, West Berlin

Chalk, heightened with white; 11¼×14⅜ in., 28·6×36·6 cm.

In front of the figure (which could also be interpreted as seated rather than kneeling) stands the platform with the astrolabe, which also appears in No. 33. From the Radowitz Collection.

26 A Madonna with a figure looking over her shoulder

Print Room, West Berlin

Chalk; verso of No. 25, trimmed to an oval shape.

27 Study for the *Virgin of Stuppach*

Chalk, the pattern of the brocade of the dress applied with brown water-colour; 12¼×11 in., 31·4×27·8 cm.

From the Savigny Collection.

28 A woman's head, three-quarter view

Print Room, West Berlin

Chalk; 10⅞×7¾ in., 27·6×19·6 cm.

29-34 Six drawings generally considered studies for two of the three lost Mainz altarpieces

These were removed by the Swedes from Mainz Cathedral in 1631 or 1632 and were—according to Sandrart, who saw them—lost in a shipwreck in the Baltic. Sandrart described the altarpieces as follows: "... in Mainz Cathedral on the left side of the choir, in three separate chapels three altar panels, each with two wings, painted inside and out. The first showed Our Lady with the infant Jesus in a cloud, with saints on Earth below in attendance. These include SS. Barbara, Cecilia, Elizabeth, Apollonia and

Ursula, all portrayed in so noble, natural, pious and correct a manner that they seem to belong to Heaven rather than Earth. The second panel had as its subject a blind hermit, crossing the frozen Rhine with his young guide. He is attacked by two bandits and killed, and falls on top of the screaming boy. It makes the beholder feel as if all this were really happening, and seems full of meaning. The third panel was less impressive than the other two . . ." (*Teutsche Akademie*, II, 3, p. 236). Sulpiz Boisserée saw a copy of the second Mainz altarpiece in 1810. It was the work of the Frankfurt painter Philipp Uffenbach, and had next to his signature that of Mathis, with the date 1520.

29 Head of a screaming figure

Print Room, West Berlin

Chalk; verso of No. 28.

The monogram in the lower right-hand corner is not original.

30 Study for a screaming figure with head thrown back

Print Room, West Berlin

Chalk, heightened with white; 9⅝×7⅞ in., 24·4×20 cm.

31 A woman standing with loosed hair, who holds a berry (?) or blossom (?) in her hand (St Dorothy?)

Print Room, West Berlin

Chalk, over grey water-colour; 12½×8½ in., 31·6×21·5 cm.

From the Savigny Collection.

32 St Catherine

Print Room, West Berlin

Chalk, heightened with white, over grey water-colour; verso of No. 31.

33 St Dorothy

Print Room, West Berlin

Chalk, heightened with white, over grey water-colour; 14⅛×10⅛ in., 35·8×25·6 cm.

47399

The infant Jesus belongs to the legend of the saint. For platform and astrolabe see No. 25. From the Savigny Collection.

34 A Virgin in the clouds

Beuningen Collection, Vierhouten

Chalk, the moon, in yellow wash, is reflected in the hem of the mantle; $12\frac{3}{4} \times 10\frac{1}{2}$ in., $32 \cdot 5 \times 26 \cdot 8$ cm.

The upper right-hand corner bears a sixteenth-century inscription: "Menz" ("Mainz"). From the Savigny Collection, later in the Koenigs Collection, Haarlem.

35 A three-headed creature, the so-called "Trias Romana" (the personification of pride, lechery and covetousness)

Print Room, West Berlin

Chalk; $10\frac{3}{4} \times 7\frac{7}{8}$ in., $27 \cdot 2 \times 19 \cdot 2$ cm.

At the foot in the middle the genuine signature: G within M.

36 Study of St John for the Tauberbischofsheim *Crucifixion*

Print Room, West Berlin

Chalk; $17\frac{1}{8} \times 12\frac{5}{8}$ in., $43 \cdot 4 \times 32$ cm.

From the Savigny Collection.

37 Portrait of a stout man, perhaps a cleric

National Museum, Stockholm

Chalk; $10 \times 7\frac{1}{2}$ in., $25 \cdot 5 \times 19$ cm.

In the upper left-hand corner a faked Dürer monogram, in the lower corner on the left, inscribed by a collector: "Albert Durer".

38 An old woman with closed eyes

Louvre, Paris

Chalk, heightened with white; $11\frac{3}{8} \times 8\frac{3}{4}$ in., $28 \cdot 8 \times 22 \cdot 4$ cm.

On the back of the drawing an old inscription: "HANS SCHENECZ MUOTTER AETATIS SUAE 71". Below: "margreit brelwiczin". Margret Prellwitz came from a patrician family in Halle.

Her son, Hans Schönitz, was a chamberlain at Cardinal Albrecht's court and was executed at his order.

39 Sketch for a *Madonna of Mercy*

National Museum, Stockholm

Pen and wash; $12\frac{3}{8} \times 9\frac{1}{4}$ in., $31 \cdot 5 \times 23 \cdot 4$ cm.

This drawing differs in medium (pen) and form (a sketch for a complete painting) from the rest of Mathis's surviving drawings and is not universally accepted as the master's work. But it seems to show similarities of style with well authenticated drawings.

Paintings

40–42 The Lindenhardt Altarpiece in the Parish Church, Lindenhardt, near Bayreuth

The outside of both wings and the back of the shrine are painted, the inside shows reliefs and carved figures. On the outside, to the left, the shrine bears the date 1503. The altarpiece was brought from Bindlach to Lindenhardt in 1685. It is not known where it stood originally, but it undoubtedly comes from the diocese of Bamberg, since the wooden figures represent the patrons of this bishopric (St Otto, the Emperor Henry and the Empress Kunigunde). It was accepted as Grünewald's work in 1926, but its genuineness has recently been questioned. In a bad state of preservation.

40 *Man of Sorrows with the Instruments of the Passion*

(On back of shrine.)

On pine; $66\frac{1}{2} \times 60\frac{1}{4}$ in., 169×153 cm.

41–42 *The Fourteen Helpers in Need*

(On wings.)

On pine; $62\frac{5}{8} \times 27$ in., $159 \times 68 \cdot 5$ cm.

On the left wing: SS. Margaret, Catherine, Barbara, Blaise, George, Pantaleon, Christopher, Eustace. On the right wing: SS. Egidius, Acacius, Cyriacus, Dionysius, Vitus, Erasmus.

43-44 *Mocking of Christ*
Pinakothek, Munich

On pine; 42⅞×28⅞ in., 109×73·5 cm. (cut at bottom).

An old inscription (most likely based on one which was there originally), "ANNO MDIII DI ... XX . . I . DECEMB.", was removed when the painting was restored in 1910. The original writing was probably on the strip cut off at the bottom of the panel, as had been customary on memorial paintings for the dead. Two seventeenth-century copies in Aschaffenburg and Hanau point to the family in question and to the place of origin. It is thought that the Aschaffenburg vidame, Johann von Kronberg, had given the panel to the priory church at Aschaffenburg in memory of his sister Apollonia, who died in December 1503. From there it came into the possession of Munich University, and was later restored.

45 *Crucifixion*
Öffentliche Kunstsammlung, Basle

On lime; 29½×21½ in., 75×54·5 cm.

Part of the left wing of a lost altarpiece. The panel first appeared in the catalogue of the Basle Collection in 1775. In the background, to the left, barely recognizable, Christ in prayer on the Mount of Olives. To the left, above, five angels' heads. To the right, in the background, soldiers leaving after the Crucifixion. It is possible that the darkness in the picture bears some relation to an eclipse in 1502. But it could also be explained by the story of the Crucifixion in the Bible.

46-58 Two fixed wings of an altarpiece given to the church of the Frankfurt Dominicans in 1509 by a member of a patrician family, Jakob Heller

The central panel was an *Assumption of the Virgin* by Dürer and was lost in a fire. The movable wings—figures of saints and the *Adoration of the Kings*—are the work of one of Dürer's pupils. They have been largely preserved and are painted in grisaille on the reverse, as are the fixed wings. Sandrart saw the complete work. He recognized the fixed wings as Grünewald's work and placed them in the year 1505. Since Dürer's central panel was only painted in 1509, Sandrart's information must be wrong, as is also his designation of the figures of individual saints. The two wings were sawn into four panels—the exact date is unknown, but it was probably in the eighteenth century— of which the two missing ones were recently discovered in private possession.

48, 50 *St Elizabeth*
Fürstl. Fürstenbergische Gemäldesammlung, Donaueschingen

On pine; 37¾×16⅞ in., 95·8×42·8 cm. (slightly cut at top and bottom).

Above the niche the branch of a fig-tree; at the feet of the saint galium, liverwort and mallow. On the back of the panel the plinth, base and shaft of a column.

49, 51 *Female Saint (St Lucy?)*
Fürstl. Fürstenbergische Gemäldesammlung, Donaueschingen

On pine; 39⅞×17¼ in., 101·2×43·7 cm. (slightly cut at top).

Above the niche a spray of periwinkle; at the feet of the saint chickweed, hawk's bit, celandine and hawkweed. The back of the panel similar to No. 48. Both panels were restored in 1952–3. The shadow thrown by the saint was largely repainted.

52, 54, 57 *St Lawrence*
Städelsches Kunstinstitut, Frankfurt am Main

On pine; 39×17 in., 99·1×43·2 cm. (slightly cut at top).

Above the saint a spray of hop, in the lower right a medlar bush. The monogram in the lower right-hand corner (G in M and N) and the name of the saint were recently proved to be later additions. On the back of the panel the shaft and ivy-wreathed capital of a column.

53, 55, 56, 58 *St Cyriacus with Princess Artemia*
Städelsches Kunstinstitut, Frankfurt am Main

35

On pine; 38⅞×17¼ in., 98·8×43·8 cm. (slightly cut at top).

Behind the saint a fig-tree. The saint's name is a later addition. The back of the panel similar to No. 52. The capital of the column is wreathed in periwinkle.

59 *Crucifixion*

Kress Collection, National Gallery, Washington
On lime; 24¼×18⅛ in., 61·5×46 cm.

For a long time, the panel was only known from an engraving by Sadler of 1605. Sandrart recognized this to have been based on a work by Grünewald. During the seventeenth century, many copies in the form of paintings and sculpture were made of this drawing (fifteen have survived to the present day). The original, at the time in the possession of William V, duke of Bavaria, was only rediscovered fairly recently in a private collection. During the restoration, the signature "m g" was uncovered at the top of the Cross.

60-122 The High Altar of the Antonite Church at Isenheim (Alsace)

Unterlindenmuseum, Colmar
Altarpiece with a shrine, two fixed and four movable wings, over a predella, which could be closed by two panels. Only a small fragment survives of the original carved surround. The carvings in the shrine—SS. Augustine, Anthony and Jerome, as well as the statues of a peasant and a shepherd—were the gift of Jean d'Orliac, preceptor of the Order, and are the work of the Strassburg sculptor Niklas Hagnower. They were completed around 1505. The sculptures of the predella—Christ and the twelve apostles—were carved by Desiderius Beichel. The wings were a later gift by Guido Guersi, who had succeeded Jean d'Orliac to the preceptorship on the former's resignation in 1490 and who stayed in office until his death in 1516. The Guersi coat of arms is shown in the hermit panel below the seated St Anthony, who probably bears the donor's features (see No. 10). There are no records of the origin of the paint-

ings; but they probably date from before Guersi's death in 1516 and are no earlier than 1511, since Mathis painted a panel (since lost) for the Frankfurt Dominicans in that year. This theory is supported by the fact that Mathis could not be called to give evidence in a court case against Hans Mertenstein (1514-15) in Frankfurt, as he was absent and probably working at Isenheim. 1515, the date on Mary Magdalene's jar, could also be the date of the *Crucifixion* panel. In addition, Mathis entered the service of Cardinal Albrecht in 1516. His work at Isenheim was probably completed by that time. It stood throughout the following centuries at its place in the choir of the Antonite church at Isenheim and was greatly admired. Many princely collectors—the Emperor Rudolf II, the Elector Maximilian of Bavaria, the Elector Frederick William I of Prussia—tried in vain to buy it. In the end, the French Revolution caused it to be removed to Colmar (1794), where it was later placed in its present setting. The artist's name was already forgotten at the end of the sixteenth century. The panels were attributed to Dürer, who represented German painting to the French conquerors of Alsace. It was Jacob Burckhardt who recognized the real creator in 1844, after Boisserée and Engelhardt had moved in the right direction. It was later established beyond doubt as Mathis's work by Woltmann's studies (1873-6).
All the panels are of lime.

60 The altar with wings closed

61 The altar with outer movable wings open

62 The altar with inner movable wings open

63 As on view at the Unterlindenmuseum, Colmar

64-67, *Lamentation*
73 (Predella; the two panels are now joined.)
26⅝×134¼ in., 67×341 cm.

68, 69, *St Anthony*

74 (On fixed left wing.)

91⅜×29½ in., 232×75 cm.

See also No. 23. Compare the attitude of the saint with that of the figure of St Anthony on Martin Schongauer's altarpiece, originally also in the Antonite church (today in the Unter-lindenmuseum, Colmar). The older work was most probably known to Mathis.

70–72 *St Sebastian*

(On fixed right wing.)

91⅜×30⅛ in., 232×76·5 cm.

See also Nos. 15, 16.

75–83 *Crucifixion*

(On outer movable wings and revealed when they are closed.)

105⅞ (at highest point)×120⅞ in., 269×307 cm.

The artist did not merely present the Crucifixion as an historical event, but as the mystery of Christ's sacrifice, with the Agnus Dei and, above all, the powerful figure of St John the Baptist—whose gesture is accompanied by the words: "Illum oportet crescere, me autem minui" (John iii, 30)—in attendance. On the jar of the prostrate Mary Magdalene is inscribed the date, 1515. Compare No. 13. As on practi-cally all of Mathis's panels, numerous corrections are evidence of his characteristically painstaking manner. Thus the head of Christ originally did not droop quite so much. The outline of the right upper arm was nearly an inch lower. Mary Magdalene stood upright, her mantle falling backwards at an angle. St John the Evangelist at first merely supported the Virgin instead of clasping her tightly. His right arm did not stretch forward to the same extent, the position of the fingers of the right hand has been changed considerably. The Virgin's eyes were open. It was not until the right hand of St John the Baptist was corrected that it assumed its significant outspread form.

84–88 *Annunciation*

(On back of left half of *Crucifixion* and revealed when outer movable wings are open.)

105⅞ (at highest point)×55⅞ in., 269×142 cm.

In front of the Virgin a book with the text: "Ecce virgo concipiet et pariet filium et voca-bitur nomen eius Emmanuel" (Isa. vii, 14). See also Nos. 9, 21.

89–102 *Christmas (Angel Concert and Nativity)*

(On inner movable wings and revealed when they are closed.)

104⅛ (at highest point)×119⅝ in., 265×304 cm.

An extensive literature exists on the symbolism of these panels, since this representation of the *Nativity* is a departure from all previous canons. It is obvious that it is no more a painting of an historical event than the *Crucifixion*, but rather a glorification of the Mother of Our Lord and an illustration of the symbolic significance of Christ's humanity. Feurstein, who was the first to point to the Revelations of St Bridget in the *Sermo angelicus* as the source not only of the *Christmas* picture but of the entire altarpiece, has also made a survey of the various interpreta-tions. They have increased considerably since. These Revelations, widely known in Germany since the appearance of the first edition in Lübeck in 1492, were published by Koberger in Nuremberg ten years later. They seem a more likely explanation of the symbolism of Mathis's work than J. Bernhart's learned liturgic inter-pretation (*Die Symbolik im Menschwerdungsbild des Isenheimer Altars*, Munich, 1921). According to Feurstein, the Virgin of the Annunciation is shown on the left kneeling at the threshold of the Old Testament, in the "House and Temple of Solomon before the new era of the fulfilment", to the right is the symbol of the New Testa-ment, "the fulfilment of the promise that God would come into the World in human form". The figure with the shining crown in the door-way of the temple can thus be explained as the "Maria aeterna, chosen by the Creator as the Mother of God before the beginning of the World, the symbol of the hopes of mankind, as described in sacred verse". The glass ewer on the step is the symbol of virginity, the vessels in the chamber of birth indicate the humiliation of Christ's descent to Earth. On the right, the Virgin of the Nativity is sitting in the *hortus conclusus*, the enclosed garden. She is the "rose without a thorn" (shown on her right), the "dwelling of the Lord" (the church in the background). The *Christmas* picture cannot be entirely explained from the Revelations of St Bridget. Mathis's imagination drew strength from many other sources, unknown to us, which were transformed and unified by his art.

103–6 *Resurrection*

(On back of right half of *Crucifixion* and revealed when outer movable wings are open.)

$105\frac{7}{8}$ (at highest point)$\times 56\frac{1}{4}$ in., 269$\times$143 cm.

107, 109–12, 114, 115 *The Meeting of St Anthony and St Paul in the Wilderness*

(On back of left half of *Christmas* picture and revealed when inner movable wings are open.)

$104\frac{1}{8}$ (at highest point)$\times 55\frac{1}{2}$ in., 265$\times$141 cm.

According to the *Golden Legend*, the ninety-year-old St Anthony found the hundred-and-thirteen-year-old St Paul, the first hermit, after searching in vain for a long time. The saint was living on water and dates and on bread, which God sent daily by means of a raven. After the two hermits had talked together, St Paul begged his visitor to bring him the mantle of St Athanasius. On his return, the visitor found St Paul dead, and buried him with the help of two lions. St Anthony, in Antonite habit, bears the features of Guido Guersi, whose coat of arms is standing against his seat. (The head of St Paul recalls No. 20, the "self-portrait". See also Nos. 17, 18.)

108, 113, 116–22 *The Temptation of St Anthony*

(On back of right half of *Christmas* picture and revealed when inner movable wings are open.)

$104\frac{1}{8}$ (at highest point)$\times 54\frac{3}{4}$ in., 265$\times$139 cm.

The interpretation of this theme is based on the well-known engraving by Martin Schongauer. In the lower right-hand corner the lament of the saint (and of the sick of the Antonite hospital at Isenheim): "Ubi eras Jhesu bone, ubi eras? Quare non affuisti, ut sanares vulnera mea?"

123–30 The Altarpiece of the Virgin of the Snow from the Collegiate Church, Aschaffenburg

In 1513 Canon Heinrich Reitzmann (1462–1528) commissioned an altarpiece with the theme of the Virgin of the Snow. In 1514 the order was repeated, with another for an altar for Oberissigheim, about which there is no other information. It was again repeated in 1517, when there is mention of the colours being in the hands of the client and of the sum of twenty-five Gulden, to be made available for the work. The frame of the altarpiece is still preserved in the chapel of the Three Kings or the Virgin of the Snow (consecrated in 1516) in the collegiate church at Aschaffenburg and bears the names of the donors, Heinrich Reitzmann and Kaspar Schantz, the date 1519, and the monogram G in M, surmounted by an N. The panels must therefore have been painted between 1517 and 1519. An altar wing, today in Freiburg im Breisgau, was beyond doubt part of the Aschaffenburg Altarpiece. Whether the large panel in Stuppach also belonged to it originally —as Schmid and many later scholars assume—is not certain, though not unlikely. But in this case the miraculous veil on the Stuppach panel, which was an object of veneration at Tauberbischofsheim, would be difficult to explain. Quite early, perhaps already in Mathis's lifetime, the central panel and the two wings were removed. The former was replaced in 1577 by an *Adoration of the Kings* by Isaak Kiening of Speyer, a work of little artistic merit. The Freiburg *Miracle of the Snow* was removed from the Aschaffenburg church in 1828 to the Munich gallery, and was sold in 1852 for 15 Gulden, 36 Kreuzer. After passing through the hands of various collectors it was given to the town of Freiburg in 1904. It had been rediscovered by Bayersdorfer in 1897 as a Grunewald painting. In 1908 the *Virgin of Stuppach* was brought in Megentheim—where, according to an old tradition, it had been since the sixteenth century—by the parish priest of Stuppach. It was generally considered a work of Rubens throughout the nineteenth century, and has only been clearly re-established as Mathis's work since 1907.

123-5 *The Miracle of the Snow*

(On right wing of the Aschaffenburg Altar-piece.)

Augustinermuseum, Freiburg im Breisgau

On pine partly covered with canvas; 70½×36 in., 179×91·5 cm.

On the back the right-hand section of an *Adoration of the Kings* from another, weaker hand. The feast of the Virgin of the Snow, widely celebrated in Germany, had been introduced in Mainz by Archbishop Uriel von Gemmingen. Heinrich Reitzmann, the donor of the altar, had written a pamphlet (Basle, 1515) advocating its celebration. The painting is based on the legend of the earliest Roman church dedicated to the Virgin. As they lay asleep on the night of August 3, 352, the Roman patrician John—who thought of donating a church—and Pope Liberius both dreamed that freshly fallen snow would mark the spot for a church. John, his wife, and the pope really found snow the next morning and had the basilica of Santa Maria Maggiore built there. The painting shows the dreaming pope in his bed on the left, while John and his wife stand in front of the building and admire the apparition of the Virgin in the sky. The faithful are stepping from the Lateran basilica in the background to admire the miracle. To the right can be seen a crowd and a procession of the clergy, headed by the pope, who marks the place for the new church in the snow, next to the kneeling figures of the Roman couple. Schmid had already indicated that the architecture was based on old Roman views. It is roughly the view from Santa Maria Maggiore to the Lateran palace and the Lateran basilica. The latter's transept and a gate in the old Roman city wall can be seen in the background.

126-30 *The Virgin of Stuppach*

Parish Church, Stuppach, near Mergentheim (Württemberg)

On pine covered with canvas; 72⅞×59 in., 185×150 cm.

A representation of "the Mother of Our Lord as guardian of a church in great peril" (Zülch). The rainbow and the church are symbols from the Revelations of St Bridget. The north front of Strassburg Cathedral as it looked in 1520 is clearly recognizable. The beehives and the closed gate in the background belong to the symbolism of the Madonna, the fig-tree on the left stands for Christ. See also No. 27.

131-4 *The Meeting of St Erasmus and St Maurice*

Pinakothek, Munich

On pine; 89×69¼ in., 226×176 cm.

Mentioned 1525 in the inventory of the colle-giate church, Halle. In 1540 it was taken to Aschaffenburg with other treasures from the priory church by its donor, Cardinal Albrecht von Brandenburg, to protect it from the distur-bances of the Reformation. During the seven-teenth century it was kept in the local castle; in 1836 it was brought to the Alte Pinakothek in Munich with the other requisitioned art treasures. It had been valued at 3,000 Gulden in an inventory of 1829, an extraordinarily high sum for the period. St Erasmus has the features of Cardinal Albrecht. At his feet are the arms of the religious foundations of Mainz, Magde-burg and Halberstadt. Harness and headgear of St Maurice are exact replicas of a silver statuette in the church treasure of Halle.

135-42 *Crucifixion* and *Christ carrying the Cross*, from Tauberbischofsheim

Kunsthalle, Karlsruhe

Front and back of a panel, separated in 1883. *Crucifixion.* On pine; 75⅝×59⅞ in., 192×152 cm. *Christ carrying the Cross.* On pine; 76×59½ in., 193×151 cm.

Perhaps from the Tauberbischofsheim church (demolished in 1664). Hans Thoma noticed the panel in 1873. It was afterwards rediscovered

39

at a gilder's in Tauberbischofsheim by the director of the Cassel gallery, Eisenmann (1877) and sold to the collector Habich. The restoration in 1883 revealed the later painting of *Christ carrying the Cross* at the back. The panel was brought back to Tauberbischofsheim in 1889 and was purchased at a price of 40,000 marks for the Karlsruhe gallery in 1899. The original setting of the panel is unknown.

143 *Lamentation*

Collegiate Church, Aschaffenburg

On pine; $14\frac{1}{8} \times 53\frac{1}{2}$ in., 36×136 cm.

Origin and date of the work not clearly established. On the left the arms of Cardinal Albrecht von Brandenburg, on the right those of Archbishop Dietrich von Erbach (d. 1459). Sulpiz Boisserée did not notice the panel on his visit to the church in 1810. It was possibly taken from another church and put there later.

Missing works by Mathis Gothardt Neithardt, of which there is documentary evidence (after the catalogues of H. A. Schmid and W. K. Zülch).

Only works after 1503 are mentioned, since it is quite likely that earlier reports refer to another "Master Mathis". Panels referred to in the literature on Grünewald but whose existence is problematical have been omitted from this list.

1 Central panel, right wing and lower portion of the left wing of an altarpiece, of which the Basle *Crucifixion* was part (No. 45). Probably a representation of the Passion.

2 *Coronation of the Virgin*. The Virgin is standing in the clouds, one angel holds the train of her mantle, a second the Earth with the infant Jesus, who is crowning his Mother. A seventeenth-century woodcut copy bears the monogram G in M and a date, 1510 (Zülch's fig. 205).

3 The *Transfiguration on Mount Tabor*, mentioned by Sandrart as the property of the Dominicans at Frankfurt am Main. See Nos. 2–8.

4 Altar for Oberissigheim, ordered by Heinrich Reitzmann in 1514. It is doubtful whether it was executed. It was supposed to show the Mater Gloriosa in the centre, to the right St Vincent, to the left St Jerome, and St George on horseback below.

5 *Mary Magdalene lamenting the dead Christ.* Known from a copy of 1648 (Fürstl. Fürstenbergische Gemäldesammlung, Donaueschingen). The work was either a wing of the Magdalene Altarpiece from the north chapel of the Antonite church at Isenheim—Guido Guersi was buried in front of this altar in 1516—or a wing from the Magdalene Altarpiece in the priory church in Halle. The second theory seems more likely, since the Isenheim Altarpiece of Mary Magdalene has recently come to be considered a work of the school of Schongauer. The copy indicates that it is a late work.

6 Left wing of the Virgin of the Snow Altarpiece in Aschaffenburg. The right wing is in Freiburg im Breisgau (Nos. 123–5), the central panel was either the Stuppach panel (Nos. 126–30) or another composition, to which the sketch for a *Madonna of Mercy* (No. 39) might belong.

7–9 The three Mainz altarpieces, supposedly removed by the Swedes. It is by no means certain that these altarpieces were lost in a shipwreck, as Sandrart claimed. Zülch holds that the panels seen—but, strangely, not described, contrary to his habit—by Sandrart at the house of the Swedish Resident in The Hague, Peter Spiering, were parts of the Mainz altarpieces. For the subjects see notes on Nos. 29–34.

10, 11 Two panels, listed in the Frankfurt inventory of Mathis's goods. One showed the crucified Christ with the Virgin and St John.

12 Full-size painting of St John the Evangelist, looking up to the Cross with folded hands. Discovered in the possession of Pope Urban VIII at Castel Gandolfo between 1630 and 1632 by Sandrart, and marked by him "Mathaeus Grunwald Alemann fecit", since it had previously been attributed to Dürer.

13 Several panels from the Peter Spiering Collection in The Hague. Perhaps parts of the Mainz altarpieces (see 7–9 above).

14 An altarpiece, which included the surviving Aschaffenburg *Lamentation* (No. 143). Perhaps a *Crucifixion*.

15 An altarpiece, of which the Tauberbischofsheim panel formed a part (Nos. 135–42). Probably the theme of the Passion.

INDEX OF PLACES

Note: Drawings indicated with an asterisk were formerly in the collections listed here; their present location is uncertain. When the artist has made drawings on both sides of a single sheet of paper, the two titles are bracketed together. The numbers are those of the plates.

PHOTOGRAPHIC SOURCES

Most of the photographs were specially taken for reproduction in this book by Walter Dräyer, Zürich, Hans Hinz, Basle (colour plates), and Martin Hürlimann, Zürich.

Other photographs were kindly placed at our disposal by:

Ashmolean Museum, Oxford, 14
Bayrisches Landesamt für Denkmalpflege, Munich, 40, 41, 42
Direktion Bayrischer Staatsgemäldesammlungen, Munich, 43, 131, 134
Graphische Sammlung der Universitätsbibliothek, Erlangen, 20
Haus der Rheinischen Heimat, Cologne, 59
Hessische Treuhandverwaltung, Wiesbaden, 29
Museum Boymans, Rotterdam, 34
National Museum, Stockholm, 37, 39
Reinhardt Collection, Winterthur (Photo Wullschleger), 13
Staatliche Kunstsammlungen, Weimar, 10
Staatliche Museen zu Berlin, 2, 3, 4, 30
Städelsches Kunstinstitut, Frankfurt am Main (Photo Hauck), 46, 47, 52, 53, 54, 55
Town Museum, Aschaffenburg, 143
Walter Steinkopf, Berlin, 30

THE PLATES

DER HERR SEGNE DICH
VND BEHVTE DICH
DER HERR LASSE
SEIN ANGESICHT
LEVCHTEN VBER
DIR VND SEI DIR
GENEDIG
DER HERR HEBE SEIN
ANGESICHT VBER DICH
VND GEBE DIR FRIEDE
ICH LEGE EVCH HEVTE
FVR DEN SEGEN VND DEN
FLVCH DEN SEGEN SO IR
GEHORCHET DEN GEBOTEN
DES HERREN EWRS GOTTES
DEN FLVCH ABER SO IR NIT
GEHORCHEN WERDET
VERFLVCHT SEI WER EIN GOC
ZEN ODER GEGOSSEN BILD
MACHT EIN GREVEL DES HERR
VERFLVCHT SEI   VATER
VND MVTTER

2

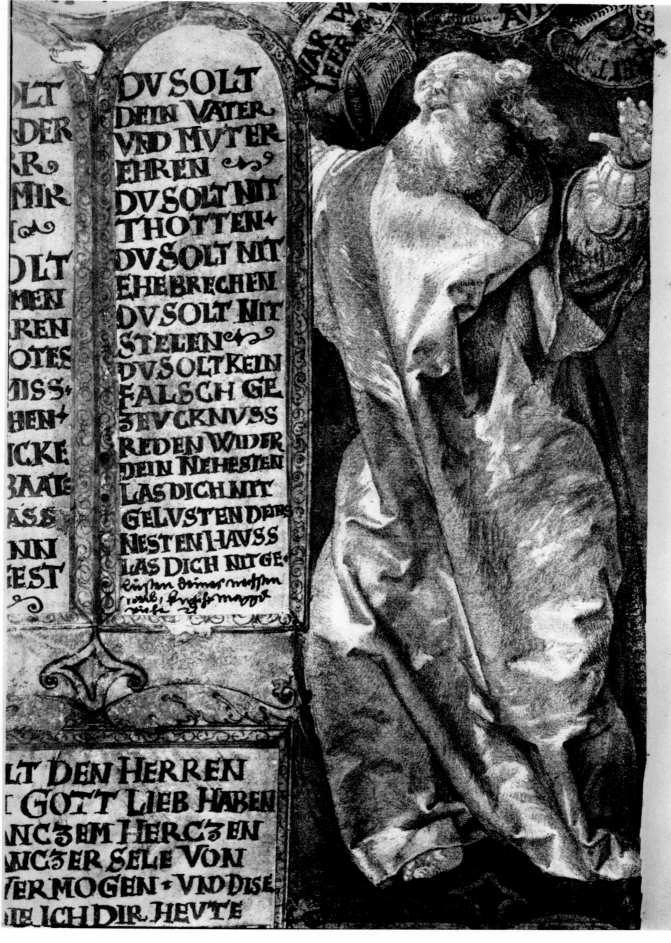

DV SOLT
DEIN VATER
VND MVTER
EHREN
DV SOLT NIT
THOTTEN
DV SOLT NIT
EHEBRECHEN
DV SOLT NIT
STELEN
DV SOLT KEIN
FALSCH GE
ZEVGKNVSS
REDEN WIDER
DEIN NEHESTEN
LAS DICH NIT
GELVSTEN DEINS
NESTEN HAVSS
LAS DICH NITGE

OLT
DER
R
MIR
A
OLT
MEN
REN
OTES
VSS
HEN
ICKE
RAAT
ASS
NN
EST

LT DEN HERREN
T GOTT LIEB HABEN
NCZEM HERCZEN
NCZER SELE VON
ERMOGEN VND DISE
IE ICH DIR HEVTE

3

GESANDT HAST IHESVM CHRIST ERKENNE

AVCH FIEL AN
ZEICHEN THET I
VOR SEINEN IV
DIE NIT GESCHI
SINT IN DISEM I
DISE ABER SIN
SCHRIBEN DAS
GLAVBET IHES
SEI CHRIST DER
GOTTES VND DA
DVRCH DEN GL
DAS LEBEN HA
IN SEINEM NAM
DIS IST DER IVN
DER VON DISEN I
ZEVGET VND HA
GESCHRIBEN V
WIR WISSEN I
SEIN ZEVGNIS V
HAFTIG IST＊IO＊

4

ACH DAS SIE EIN SOLICH HERCZ HETTEN
MICH ZV FVRCHTEN VND ZV HALTEN ALLE
MEINE GEBOT IR LEBEN LANCK AVF DAS
INEN WOL GINGE VND IREN KINDERN
EWIGLICH
O WELCH EIN VATERLICHS HERCZ

5

6

7

9

12

13

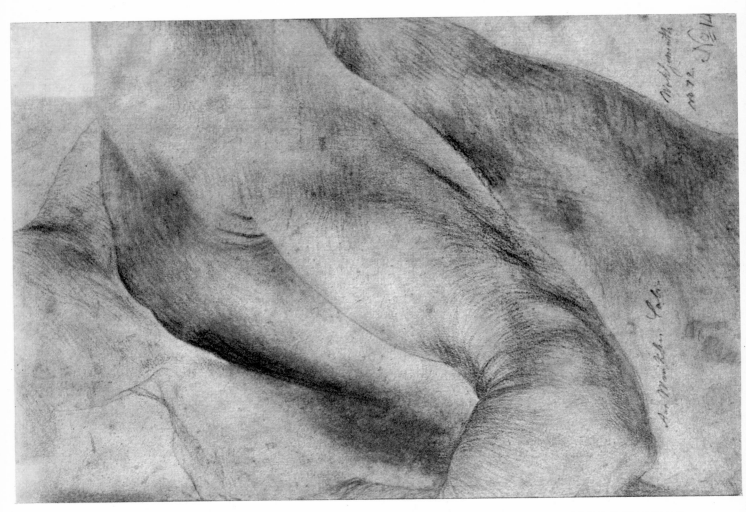

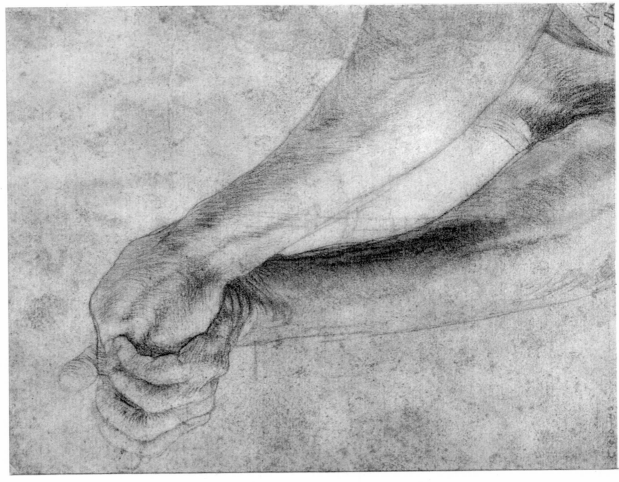

15

19

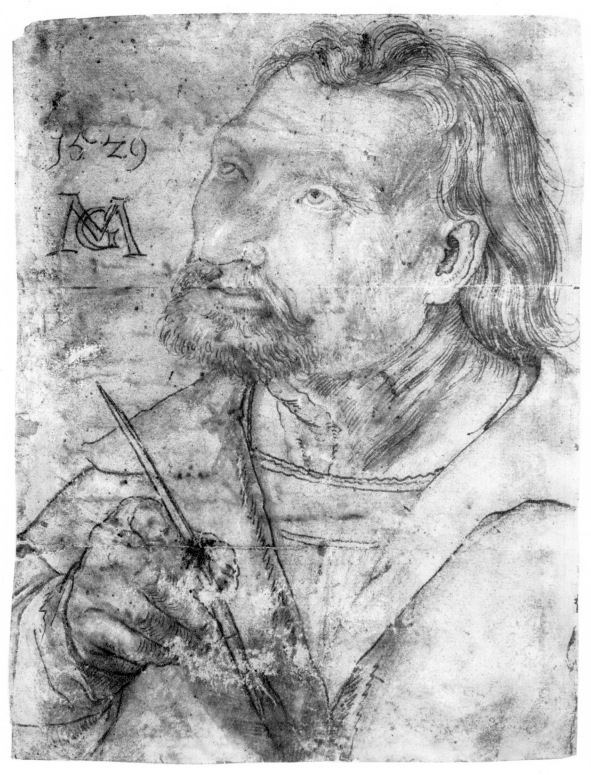

20

21

22

N? 183

23

25

26

N° 180.

27

K.l.Z. 1070

28

29

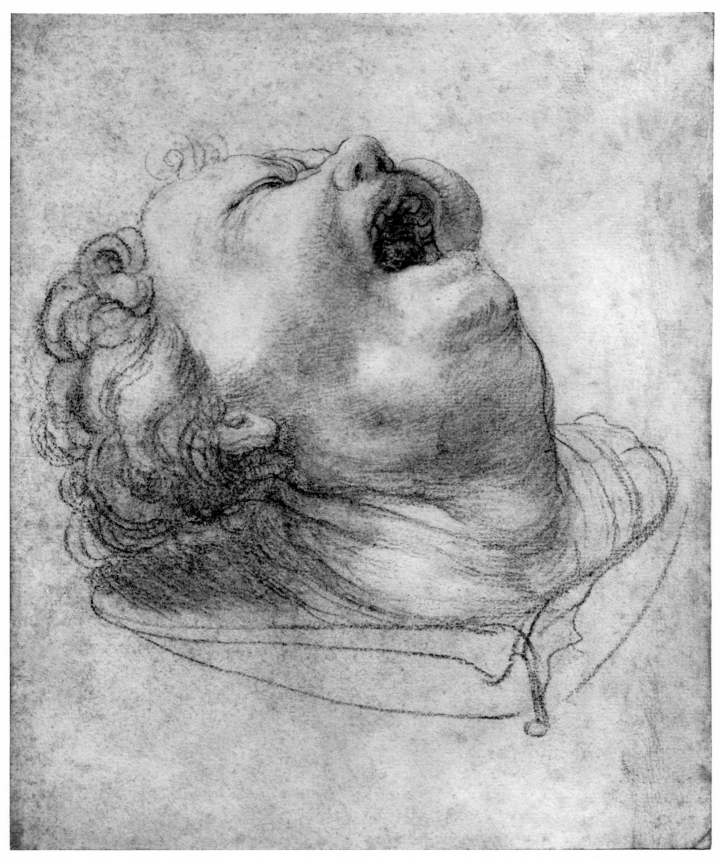

30

31

32

№ 177

33

№ 176

34

35

albert Durer. 1644

37

38

39

40

42

46

47

48

S · CIRIACVS ·

53

56

57

58

59

60

61

62

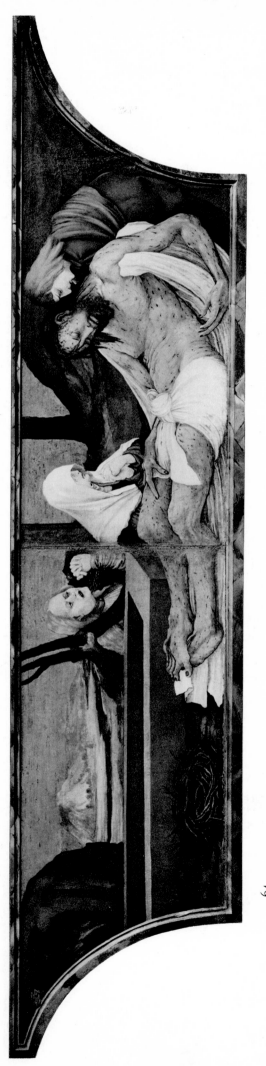

67

73

74

77

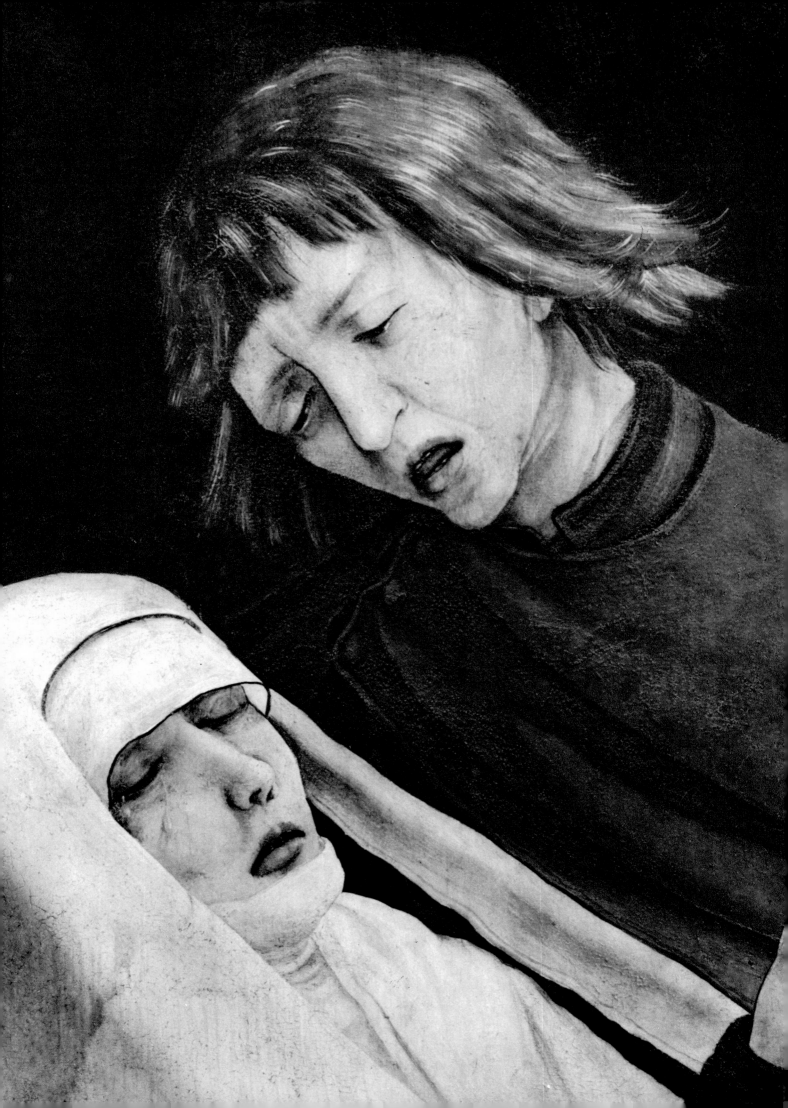

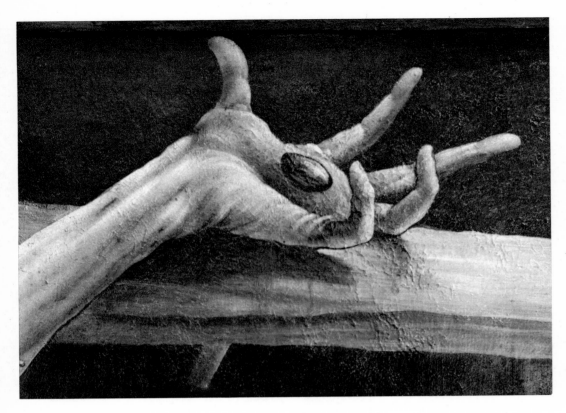

81

82

86

87

90

93

94

105

106

112

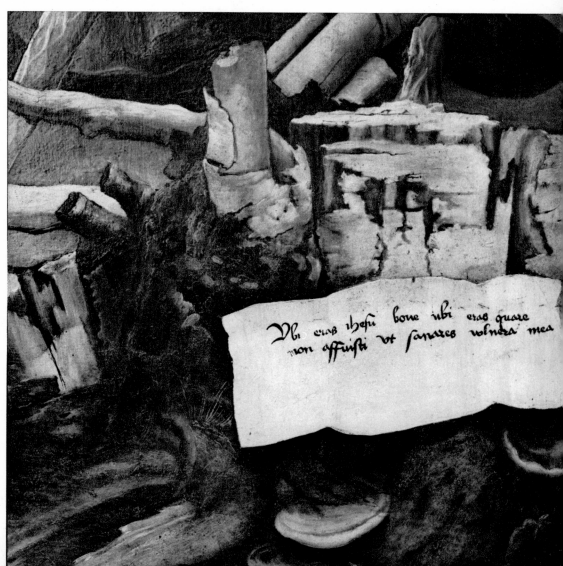

Vbi eras ihesu bone ubi eras quare
non affuisti vt sanares vulnera mea

116

117

118

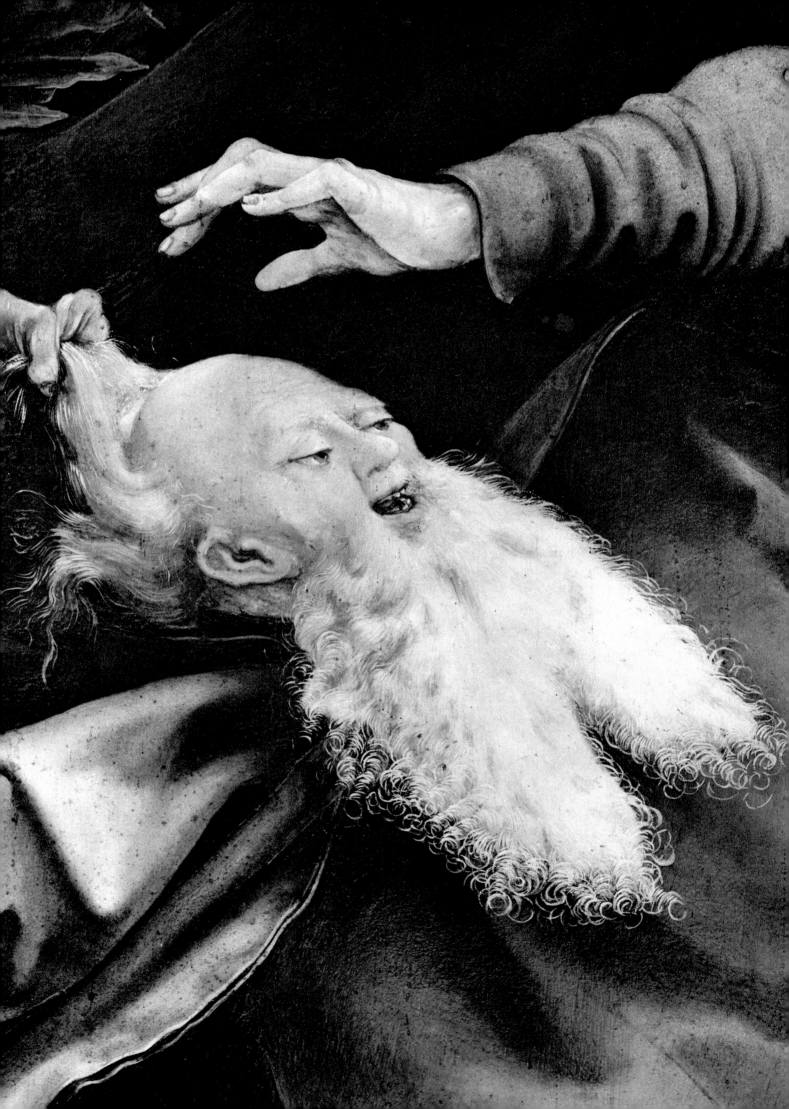

128

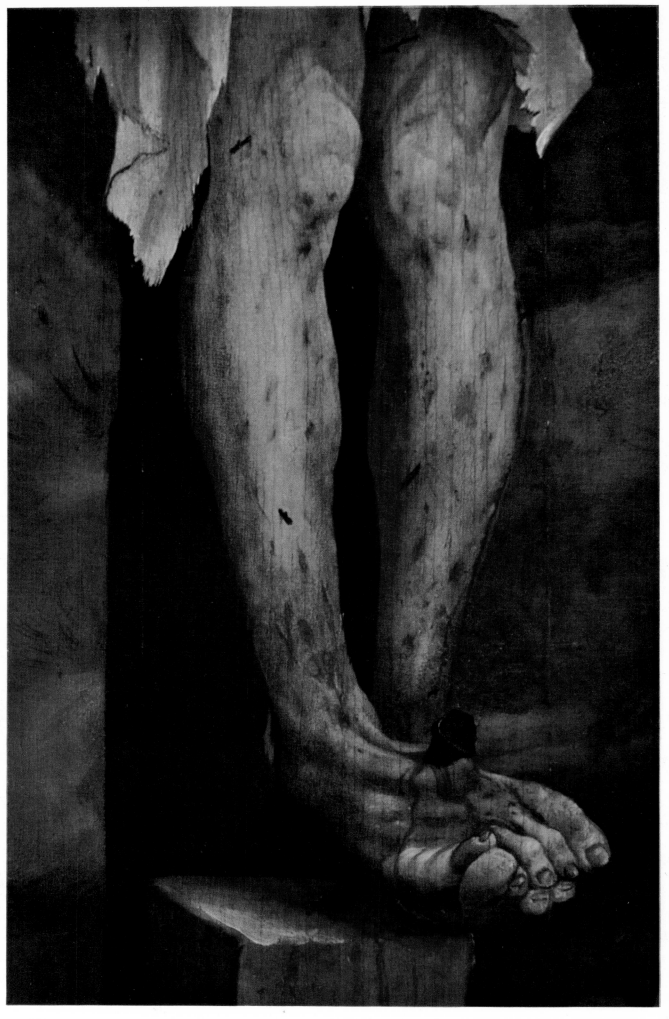